Budgeting
for Hard Power

Budgeting
for Hard Power

Defense and Security Spending
Under Barack Obama

MICHAEL E. O'HANLON

BROOKINGS INSTITUTION PRESS
Washington, D.C.

Library of Congress Cataloging-in-Publication data

O'Hanlon, Michael E.
 Budgeting for hard power : defense and security spending under Barack
Obama / Michael E. O'Hanlon.
  p. cm.
 Includes bibliographical references and index.
 Summary: "Lays out the issues and relative costs facing the new president:
prioritizing among competing demands for defense spending, homeland-
security investment, diplomacy, and security assistance; determining how much
money will be needed, available, and allocated. Suggests a path for the new
White House in its resource-allocation decisions affecting U.S. national
security"—Provided by publisher.
 ISBN 978-0-8157-0294-8 (pbk. : alk. paper)
  1. Obama, Barack. 2. National security—United States—Finance.
3. United States—Armed Forces—Appropriations and expenditures. 4. United
States. Dept. of Defense—Appropriations and expenditures. 5. United States.
Dept. of Homeland Security—Appropriations and expenditures. 6. United
States. Dept. of State—Appropriations and expenditures. 7. United States—
Politics and government—2009– 8. United States—Military policy. 9. United
States—Foreign relations—2009– 10. Budget—United States. I. Title.

 UA23.O385 2009
 355.6'2280973—dc22   2009018697

9 8 7 6 5 4 3 2 1

The paper used in this publication meets minimum requirements of the
American National Standard for Information Sciences—Permanence of Paper
for Printed Library Materials: ANSI Z39.48-1992.

Typeset in Sabon

Composition by Cynthia Stock
Silver Spring, Maryland

Printed by R. R. Donnelley
Harrisonburg, Virginia

FOR

BOB REISCHAUER

CONTENTS

CHAPTER ONE

INTRODUCTION

THESE ARE EXTRAORDINARY TIMES in American national security policy. The nation remains involved in two of the longest conflicts of its history in Iraq and Afghanistan, with more than 4,000 lives lost over six years in Iraq and more than 600 lost over nearly eight years in Afghanistan, as well as cumulative costs approaching, to date, $700 billion in the former case and $200 billion in the latter.[1] Thankfully the prognosis in Iraq appears far improved in recent years; 2009 and 2010 will be momentous times in Afghanistan as the United States doubles combat forces there in hopes of turning around the direction of the conflict. Yet, despite this wartime focus, President Bush's second secretary of defense and President Obama's first, Robert Gates, has seemed almost as interested in helping the Department of State get funding for its units focused on nation building and stabilization missions as in lobbying for Department of Defense (DoD) resources. In his words, "It has become clear that America's civilian institutions of diplomacy and development have been chronically undermanned and underfunded for far too long."[2] He also warns against "next-war-itis" among military planners, many of whom still prefer traditional high-technology modernization programs rather than generating adequate resources for immediate needs in what was called by the Bush administration the war on terror.[3]

1

The contemporary American national security debate has evolved in other important ways as well. For example, official Pentagon doctrine now formally considers nation building, stabilization, and peacekeeping missions just as central to its portfolio as deterring or defeating traditional enemy combatants. At a more operational level, when coaching his troops, the country's star general in Iraq, David Petraeus, emphasized restraint in the use of force as much as destruction of the enemy. In another domain of national security policy, several former secretaries of state and defense, including Republicans and Democrats, advocate the eventual elimination of all nuclear weapons on the planet. And with the Taiwan issue fairly quiet at present, security discussions about China now focus as much on our common interest in ensuring reliable energy supplies and preventing global warming as on preparing for scenarios that would pit our forces against each other.

But for all this shifting of tectonic plates in the national security debate, those anticipating a radical change in actual American national security policy under President Obama should not leap to conclusions. The Pentagon budget was not a major source of contention in last year's presidential race—because neither candidate had any real interest in proposing that it be cut (despite the fact that, even excluding war costs, it exceeds the cold war average in real-dollar or inflation-adjusted terms; see figures 1-1 and 1-2). President Obama is committed to ending the Iraq war but also, as noted, to beefing up U.S. efforts in Afghanistan, including a promised increase in deployed U.S. troops in that theater. Eventual nuclear weapons abolition may now be the goal, but no one knows how to achieve such a dramatic, absolute goal in the coming years. Slowing nuclear proliferation where possible on a case by case basis, strengthening homeland security measures, gradually deploying missile defenses, and resuming the slog of formal arms control seem a more likely future action agenda for the country's nuclear specialists. And the current state of the Taiwan issue notwithstanding, the rise of China, while welcome in so many ways for the world and the United States, nonetheless inherently constitutes a latent national security issue for this country. War against China is very unlikely, and the magnitude of China's military threat to the United States needs to be kept in perspective.[4] But addressing the strategic implications of China's growing wealth and military power must be a main focus for U.S. strategists nonetheless—in part

FIGURE 1-1. Department of Defense Annual Budget Authority, 1948–2014[a]

Billions of 2009 dollars

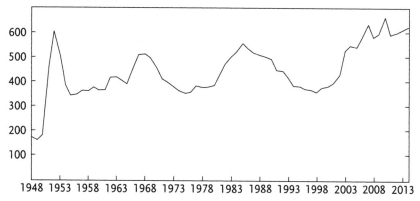

Source: For years 1948–2008: U.S. Department of Defense, *National Defense Budget Estimates for FY 2009* (Washington, updated September 2008), pp. 109–14. For years 2009–14: Office of Management and Budget, *A New Era of Responsibility: Renewing America's Promise* (U.S. Government Printing Office, 2009), pp. 130–31.

a. Amounts are in constant FY 2009 dollars. The Department of Defense estimate for FY 2010 includes a proposed $130 billion for Overseas Contingency Operations. Such estimates for FY 2011–2014 are currently $50 billion per annum.

to ensure that the chances of war remain small in a future where Taiwan may again become a flash point.

The age of the advertised preemption doctrine may be over, and the tools of American soft power may be likely to receive an infusion of resources in the new administration. But the end of preemption policy has greater implications for foreign policy, and for decisions on the use of force, than for defense budgeting or national security resource allocation. That is because rapid response will remain a necessary capability for the United States with or without such a nominal doctrine. President Obama will have to spend a great deal of time and money on national security, hard power, and war as well.

This book is designed to help policymakers wrestle with resource allocation decisions affecting the national security of the United States. Previous Brookings books on U.S. national security budgets have focused almost exclusively on the Pentagon and on Department of Energy (DOE) nuclear weapons programs. This study has a broader

FIGURE 1-2. **Department of Defense, Budget Authority by Service, FY 1960–2013**[a]

Percent

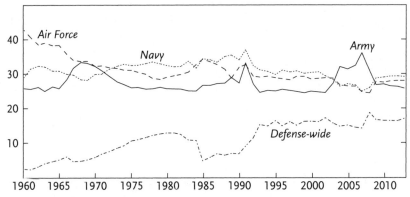

Source: U.S. Department of Defense, *National Defense Budget Estimates for FY 2009* (Washington, updated September 2008), pp. 67–72.

a. For 1991, the official percentage of the budget authority for "Defense-wide" spending was –3 percent. This was due to foreign contributions to Operation Desert Storm. This is not depicted in the graph above as the curve was flattened between the years 1990 and 1992.

purview, one that also considers homeland security resources and selected parts of the State Department and foreign operations budgets. Funds for these latter activities are also crucial for American security, in part as a result of 9/11 and the wars in Iraq and Afghanistan. Rather than being about the defense budget, therefore, this book might be thought of as addressing the nation's *hard power* budget—the broader set of instruments with direct and near-term bearing on national security, including ongoing military operations and the stability and security of crucial countries around the world.

There are limits on my scope. The book does not generally extend to development aid, trade policy, or energy policy despite their significance for American national security, at least indirectly and over the longer term.[5] But in an age characterized by the terrorist threat, homeland security and State Department instruments for helping stabilize weak states cannot be ignored even in a relatively narrowly construed study.

All of my analyses in this book are influenced by the country's enormously problematic fiscal situation. The United States has real national security needs that require resources. The nation is also (still) rich and can afford what is truly needed. But I take it as a given that the federal deficit is too high and that the country's deficits are relevant to its economic future and thus its long-term national security. There is an argument, as Martin Feldstein and others have emphasized, for including defense spending as part of any short-term stimulus packages—bearing in mind that recruiting troops and buying large-ticket weaponry tends to take many months, if not years, meaning that the short-term effects of some types of military spending are often modest. The greater challenge, however, is in figuring out how national security efforts can remain robust in the future even as the nation ultimately seeks to tighten its fiscal belt after the recession is over. And that belt tightening is likely to be painful; the Obama administration is currently the relative optimist on future deficit projections in relation to the Congressional Budget Office (CBO), and it projects the following annual deficits for 2009 and beyond (sequentially): $1.75 trillion, $1.17 trillion, $912 billion, $581 billion, $533 billion, $570 billion, $583 billion, $637 billion, and so on.[6]

For these reasons, Defense, State, and Homeland Security budgets should be as frugal as possible. That is one key philosophy behind this book. The other is that resources for national security capabilities in the Department of State and Department of Homeland Security (DHS) should be selectively increased to compensate for systematic underfunding over the years.

I do not attempt here the Herculean, if not intractable, task of comparing quantitatively the likely value of investing a marginal dollar in port security relative to fighter aircraft or relative to development or security assistance. Available methods of analysis are too imprecise to make such a venture feasible in a meaningful way. For example, it is too hard to estimate the odds of a terrorist group trying to smuggle a nuclear weapon into the United States under different assumptions about border security, and too difficult to know just how much deterrence of a possible Chinese attack on Taiwan is strengthened by the purchase of additional F-22 aircraft or missile defense systems. Rather, proposals for changes in policy here are based on case-by-case assessments of likely threats, as well as the likely effectiveness of possible responses.

An underlying assumption in this book is that U.S. defense priorities are not unreasonable in their basic thrust today. They are, at present, rather balanced, focused not only on winning current wars in Iraq and Afghanistan but on deterring and preparing for possible future conflicts of uncertain and unknowable type and number. For example, dissuading

China from attacking Taiwan seems less pressing today than even a couple of years ago, but the basic American policy of engagement combined with deterrence seems to be working in that part of the world and should not be discarded. Deterrence of North Korea is still wise, given its potential for further nuclear breakout not to mention brinkmanship against South Korea—even if the chances of war have likely diminished a great deal over the decades. Deterrence of Russia is to my mind a lower priority given the unlikelihood of major war (and questionable advisability of any American military response to small wars such as that between Russia and Georgia in the summer of 2008). But with Russia's resurgence under Vladimir Putin, there is some additional and indirect benefit from a strong American military for helping stabilize Eastern Europe. A number of other scenarios with serious potential implications for American security, ranging from a possible crisis between India and Pakistan to internal unrest in a strategically crucial state like Pakistan to civil conflict in a number of African states, could conceivably also require U.S. military forces—operating on their own or, more likely, as part of a coalition. These and other considerations argue for a broad range of American military capabilities.

Current U.S. defense policy, including formal alliances or security commitments with more than sixty countries as well as major troop commitments in East Asia, Europe, the Persian Gulf, Central Asia and elsewhere, already addresses a wide portfolio of possible missions. This is appropriate. As such, my goal is less to devise a fundamentally different paradigm for U.S. national security policy than to make better choices within the broad parameters of the current paradigm. The exception to this generally conservative approach is, as noted, to emphasize the nonmilitary tools of foreign policy somewhat more than has been the case of late.

The net effects of my proposed changes would amount to no notable change in overall national security funding relative to what late Bush administration policy implies. More specifically, almost $10 billion would be cut from the Pentagon's annual budget (relative to plans that President Obama inherited). About $2.75 billion would be added for homeland security and about $7.5 billion added for what I term hard power aspects of diplomacy and foreign assistance. The defense budget would still have to grow faster than inflation, but only at the real rate of 1 to 2 percent a year in contrast with a rate of about 3 to 4 percent a year that would be required absent my suggested economies. The specifics are summarized in table 1-1 and developed throughout the rest of the book. Most could be implemented quickly. However, some could take three to four years to phase in, and some of the nuclear-related proposals would be contingent on first reaching an agreement with Russia. (The fact that many savings would take a couple of years to be realized is actually desirable at this economic moment, given the short-term need to stimulate the economy.) Cost savings are based primarily on various federal budget documents and CBO analyses.

The Obama administration has a similar plan for defense to what I propose here. The administration appears to envision budget growth in the base defense budget, not counting war costs, roughly equal to the rate of inflation over the next five years (slightly less than what I project as necessary). The Obama administration proposes a Department of Defense budget for 2010 of $534 billion that would represent 4 percent nominal growth—projected as close to 3 percent real growth—in the base defense budget. But for 2010 at least, the effective real growth is closer to zero, since some of that additional funding is to bring some functions back into the base budget that had been in supplemental appropriations during the Bush years. Projections by the House Budget Committee suggest no real growth after 2010. And Secretary Gates has offered an initial plan, before a more comprehensive Quadrennial Defense Review (QDR) to be released in February of 2010, to cut back on a number of weapons systems in a fashion similar to what I propose. Specifically, Gates would stop further production of airborne laser aircraft, end the C-17 and F-22 production programs, cancel the DDG-1000 destroyer (after building up to three more) as well as the vehicles associated with the Army's Future Combat System, defer development of a new bomber, cancel the transformational communications satellite program and the VH-71 presidential helicopter, and increase some elements of ground-based missile defense as well as the DDG-51 destroyer program. He would also accelerate the F-35 program somewhat. He would slow down aircraft carrier production resulting ultimately in a reduction of the fleet size from 11 to 10 ships, though the fleet size would not change until 2040.[7] Gates's proposed cutbacks will not suffice to achieve the goal of zero real growth, however, so the QDR will have to find more cuts, or the defense budget topline will have to increase.

There are numerous differences in specifics between the Obama administration plan and my own, and most of this book was written

TABLE 1-1. Summary Table: Recommended National Security Budget Initiatives[a]

Average annual costs, expressed in millions of 2009 dollars

The 050 Budget: Department of Defense and Nuclear-Weapons-Related Department of Energy Funds	
Reductions in DoD nuclear force posture (to 1,000 warhead ceiling)	−1,500
Reductions in DoE nuclear weapons activities	−1,000
Slowing of some missile defense programs	−2,000
Creation of peace operations division in U.S. Army	3,000
Creation of Army Advisory Corps	500
Expansion of specialized, overused Army personnel and associated aircraft	750
Creation of National Guard Brigade for homeland defense, related changes	750
Expansion of specific military benefits for war veterans, others	2,000
Increased funds for tactical reconnaissance, nonlethal weapons	1,000
Scholarship programs for future defense science, business personnel	750
Reductions in F-35/Lightning II (JSF) program, satellite communications	−1,500
Reductions in Marine Corps V-22/Osprey program, presidential helicopter	−1,900
Reductions in vehicle portion of Army FCS program	−4,000
Reduction of aircraft carrier fleet by one battle group	−2,000
Reduction of attack submarine force by 8 vessels	−2,000
Reductions of surface combatant fleet using dual crews	−1,100
Cancellation of EFV amphibious vehicle, replacement with simpler design	−750
Retention of two heavy Army brigades in Europe, hardening and improving Pacific bases	−250
Net budget changes, DoD and DoE (not counting war-related costs)	−9,250

Federal Homeland Security Accounts	
Airport and airplane security initiatives ("sniffers," cargo inspections, and so on)	350
Border patrol and related activities, US-VISIT program	350
Coast Guard force structure growth	900
"COPS II" initiative to help local police forces with counterterrorism	100
Biological detectors and FDA food inspection initiatives	600
Container cargo inspection improvements	250
Hazardous cargo inspection and security initiatives	100
Improved planning capacity at DHS	100
Net budget changes, Homeland Security (exclusive of DoD costs)	2,750

The 150 Budget: Hard Power Activities of the Department of State and Foreign Assistance Agencies	
Expansion of peacekeeping training for foreign militaries	400
Nonproliferation initiatives (some could be in the 050 budget instead)	500
Expansion of diplomatic capabilities at State	1,000
Public diplomacy efforts including increased scholarships	800
Expansion of AID/PRT capacity (in same or separate agency)	1,000
Expansion of flexible funds for ESF	200
Afghanistan security and economic aid expansion	1,700
Pakistan security and economic aid expansion	1,750
Net budget changes, hard power aspects of 150 budget	7,350

DoD = Department of Defense; DoE = Department of Energy; DHS = Department of Homeland Security; ESF = Economic Support Fund; FCS = Future Combat System; FDA = Food and Drug Administration; JSF = Joint Strike Fighter; PRT = provincial reconstruction team; USAID = U.S. Agency for International Development.
a. Savings are listed as negative numbers.

before the Gates proposals or Obama budget framework became public. So my proposal should be viewed as an independent, if philosophically and budgetarily similar, effort.[8]

Before proceeding to specifics, a word is warranted about an increasingly popular idea that the Department of Defense be guaranteed a budget equal to at least 4 percent of the nation's gross domestic product (GDP).[9] (See figure 1-3 for DoD historical spending as a percentage of GDP.) It is not a good idea, because it would amount to conferring quasi-entitlement status upon the nation's military establishment. The armed forces do not need such help, given that the nation has supported them rather well ever since the period of the Reagan buildup. And in ten or fifteen years, if our nation can ensure its national security with a defense budget smaller than 4 percent of GDP, that would be welcome. It would be helpful to the country's fiscal situation and thus its long-term economic health.

In the short term, defense will likely remain around 4 percent of GDP anyway. But that is a practical consequence of the wars we are in. It should *not* become an immutable federal budgeting principle. The

FIGURE 1-3. Department of Defense Historical Spending as a Percentage of GDP[a]

Percent

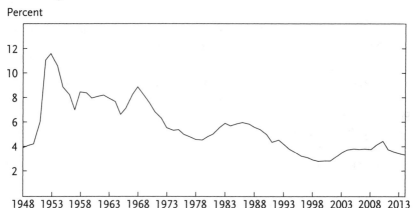

Source: For years 1948–2008: U.S. Department of Defense, *National Defense Budget Estimates for FY 2009* (Washington, updated September 2008), pp. 121–26 and 200–01. For years 2009–14: Office of Management and Budget, *A New Era of Responsibility: Renewing America's Promise* (U.S. Government Printing Office, 2009), pp. 114 and 130–31.

a. The Department of Defense estimate for FY 2010 includes a proposed $130 billion for Overseas Contingency Operations. Such estimates for FY 2011–2014 are currently $50 billion per annum.

Pentagon should be expected to argue for its budget like any other agency, not to expect a given minimum. As Secretary Gates rightly put it in 2008, "resources are scarce—and yes, it is a sign I've already been at the Pentagon for too long to say that with a straight face when talking about a half trillion dollar base budget. Nonetheless, we still must set priorities and consider inescapable tradeoffs and opportunity costs."[10]

The global economic downturn places considerable pressure on the U.S. budget, to be sure. It also poses further risks to the stability of states such as Pakistan that are of crucial importance to the United States; we cannot afford to see a nuclear-armed country with significant numbers of extremists go under.[11] But it is also worth remembering, as Richard Haass of the Council on Foreign Relations has argued, that global economic problems may hurt some of our potential adversaries too—most significantly Iran, whose dependence on oil exports makes it quite vulnerable to the rapid decline in petroleum prices that occurred in the latter part of 2008.[12] As such, it is at least possible (though hardly sure) that

Iran may prove more willing to compromise on its nuclear program during the Obama administration. In other words, one should not conclude that as a result of the global financial crisis, defense spending must automatically either go up or go down. The international economic situation must inform U.S. national security policymaking, but it should not dominate it or predetermine its conclusions.

Even with this book's broadened agenda, the Pentagon remains far and away the most expensive part of the country's national security machinery. Given current force structure and modernization programs, the CBO estimates that the peacetime defense establishment will cost an average of about $560 billion annually between 2014 and 2025 unless policy changes are made (counting Department of Energy nuclear weapons costs, expressed in constant 2009 dollars). This is almost 10 percent more than the 2009 request (again, not counting war supplementals).[13] My suggested budget would lower this average figure to about $550 billion or somewhat less, expressed in 2009 dollars. Given the magnitude of military spending, the book, therefore, devotes most of its pages to the Department of Defense, and it is with the Pentagon budget that I begin.

CHAPTER TWO

A PRIMER ON MILITARY STRATEGY, POSTURE, AND BUDGETS

MOST OF THIS BOOK is about practical resource allocation decisions. But it is first important to establish the context for these decisions.

The goals of U.S. national security remain, as they have been ever since World War II, global and ambitious. There are different ways to summarize them, depending on whether one thinks in terms of regions of the world, or types of problems, or possible military scenarios. But the objectives have included, in recent times:

—to be able to prevail in two major regional wars at once (though with somewhat changing assumptions about what those wars might entail and how fast each would be successfully concluded);

—to sustain global presence to shore up allies, deter aggressors, help preserve great-power peace, and discourage nuclear proliferation;

—to address other types of problems such as terrorism, civil conflict, and postwar stabilization and reconstruction;

—to protect the American homeland against direct attack.

The specific ways these goals have been pursued have varied; each major defense review since the cold war has had its own signature. The base force review of the first Bush administration, right after the cold war, developed the two-war framework for the first time. It also declared (through the related Defense Planning Guidance document) that an explicit goal of U.S. national security policy should be to discourage other would-be great powers from contending for global supremacy.[1] The Clinton administration's bottom-up review in 1993 did not repeat the latter goal and streamlined the two-regional-wars force structure to save money, reducing active duty uniformed personnel from about 1.6 million to 1.4 million while also cutting force structure (for example, the active Army went from twelve to ten divisions, after totaling eighteen during the Reagan years). The 1997 Quadrennial Defense Review strengthened the conceptual underpinnings of defense policy with its "shape, prepare, respond" framework. It also began to give greater emphasis to so-called asymmetric threats as well as the concept of defense revolution and transformation. But on the whole, it made just modest changes to main combat capabilities; the total size of the military went virtually unchanged.[2]

The first Rumsfeld review in 2001 tried to move away from fixation on the Persian Gulf and northeast Asia, introducing the notion of "capabilities-based planning" rather than threat-based approaches. It also argued that the United States did not need the capability to overthrow two major enemy regimes at once; a more limited operation would suffice for any second simultaneous war, it declared.[3] Released less than three weeks after the 9/11 attacks, it also elevated homeland protection to the top of the Pentagon's list of priorities. But again, words sometimes changed more than reality. The size of the active military remained at 1.4 million troops. And in fact, under the 2001 QDR, the Bush administration did overthrow two enemy regimes in very rapid succession, even though doctrinally it had just dismissed that type of scenario for planning purposes. Despite some early indications that it might cut back on ground forces fairly severely, it wound up not doing so, so force structure was largely unchanged from the Clinton years.

The 2006 review added new concepts to guide investment strategy, doctrine, and training. For example, it identified several different types of possible threats, including those deemed disruptive and catastrophic rather than just the traditional variety. But for the most part, defense policy in this period was dominated by the immediate exigencies of the ongoing Iraq and Afghanistan wars that were requiring far more resources than originally foreseen.[4] At one level, that is as it should be, even if clearly it would have been preferable to be better prepared in advance and to make any needed adjustments sooner than 2006. The basic point remains, however: prevailing in the important wars we are fighting should be priority number one for the nation's military, especially since there is little reason to think that our guard is being let down elsewhere.[5]

In fact, the 2006 review still did not do enough in this way, reflecting Mr. Rumsfeld's ongoing reluctance to fully commit to Iraq and Afghanistan. The "permanent" end-strength of the military stayed at roughly 1.4 million troops though temporary allowance was made for an increase of some 40,000 soldiers in the active Army due to the ongoing conflicts. Once he took over, Secretary Gates then authorized an overdue and larger "permanent" increase of some 92,000 ground troops, putting total military strength slightly over 1.4 million (including an active duty Army of 547,000 soldiers and an active duty Marine Corps at 202,000)—though he did so without a formal Quadrennial Defense Review decision (see table 2-1). (The use of the term *permanent* was a misnomer, since there is no such thing as a permanent size or shape to the U.S. military. What Gates did was to formalize the larger size of the Army and Marine Corps and allow funding for these larger forces to be provided out of the normal, base defense budget.)

What stands out through these twenty years is that the core objectives of U.S. national security policy listed above have continued to make sense. A two-war capability is sound on deterrence grounds. As a global power with key interests and allies around the world, the United States cannot allow the perception (or reality) that by being committed to one war in one place, it is incapable of responding elsewhere. Not only that, but this decade in particular it has been involved in two wars at once.

Unfortunately, some ideas that should have changed have not—at least not enough. More to the point, budgets have not yet shifted. The 9/11 attacks and other recent developments underscore the importance of working with allies and partners around the world not only on war fighting but on stabilization, peace operations, and nation building efforts. The United States has paid lip service to such goals, but its resource allocations have not yet reflected them meaningfully, except in the specific and special cases of supplemental appropriations for Iraq and Afghanistan—though Secretary Gates now seeks to change that with his generally sound proposals in the 2010 budget request.

Global presence also contributes to deterrence, and again, U.S. policy has been fairly steady here. Despite the prognostications of those

TABLE 2-1. U.S. Military Annual Active Duty Personnel End Strength, 1960–2009[a]

Year	Total	Army	Navy	Marines	Air Force
1960	2,492,037	877,749	624,895	175,919	813,474
1961	2,552,912	893,323	641,995	185,165	832,429
1962	2,687,690	962,712	662,837	192,049	870,092
1963	2,695,240	961,211	668,626	189,937	875,466
1964	2,690,141	972,546	670,160	189,634	857,801
1965	2,723,800	1,002,427	690,162	198,328	832,883
1966	3,229,209	1,310,144	740,646	280,641	897,778
1967	3,411,931	1,468,754	749,299	299,501	894,377
1968	3,489,588	1,516,973	759,163	308,138	905,314
1969	3,449,271	1,514,223	764,867	311,627	858,554
1970	2,983,868	1,293,276	677,152	246,153	767,287
1971	2,626,785	1,050,425	615,767	204,738	755,855
1972	2,356,301	849,824	593,135	199,624	713,718
1973	2,231,908	791,460	566,653	192,064	681,731
1974	2,157,023	784,128	546,464	192,174	634,257
1975	2,104,795	775,301	532,270	195,683	601,541
1976	2,083,581	782,668	527,781	189,851	583,281
1977	2,074,543	782,246	529,895	191,707	570,695
1978	2,062,404	771,624	530,253	190,815	569,712
1979	2,027,494	758,852	523,937	185,250	559,455
1980	2,050,826	777,036	527,352	188,469	557,969
1981	2,082,897	781,473	540,502	190,620	570,302
1982	2,108,612	780,391	552,996	192,380	582,845
1983	2,123,349	779,643	557,573	194,089	592,044
1984	2,138,157	780,180	564,638	196,214	597,125
1985	2,151,032	780,787	570,705	198,025	601,515
1986	2,169,112	780,980	581,119	198,814	608,199
1987	2,174,217	780,815	586,842	199,525	607,035
1988	2,138,213	771,847	592,570	197,350	576,446
1989	2,130,229	769,741	592,652	196,956	570,880
1990	2,046,144	732,403	581,856	196,652	535,233
1991	1,986,259	710,821	570,966	194,040	510,432
1992	1,807,177	610,450	541,883	184,529	470,315
1993	1,705,103	572,423	509,950	178,379	444,351
1994	1,610,490	541,343	468,662	174,158	426,327
1995	1,518,224	508,559	434,617	174,639	400,409
1996	1,471,722	491,103	416,735	174,883	389,001
1997	1,438,562	491,707	395,564	173,908	377,385
1998	1,406,830	483,880	382,338	173,142	367,470
1999	1,385,703	479,426	373,046	172,641	360,590

(continued)

TABLE 2-1 (*continued*)

Year	Total	Army	Navy	Marines	Air Force
2000	1,384,338	482,170	373,193	173,321	355,654
2001	1,385,116	480,801	377,810	172,934	353,571
2002	1,411,634	486,542	383,108	173,733	368,251
2003	1,434,377	499,301	382,235	177,779	375,062
2004	1,426,836	499,543	373,197	177,480	376,616
2005	1,389,394	492,728	362,941	180,029	353,696
2006	1,384,968	505,402	350,197	180,416	348,953
2007	1,379,551	522,017	337,547	186,492	333,495
2008	1,401,757	543,645	332,228	198,505	327,379

Source: Department of Defense, "Military Personnel Statistics" website (http://siadapp. dmdc.osd.mil/personnel/MILITARY/Miltop.htm).

a. Figures are as of September 30 for each year, which corresponds to the end of the fiscal year.

heralding a modern revolution in military affairs, defense technology is not changing fast enough to allow U.S. forces to be quickly deployed from the homeland to distant places in decisive quantities. For key regions, continual presence is the best way to show resolve—and it is also the only means of dependably having enough combat power available to respond quickly to suddenly developing crises. This is important not only for dealing with small extremist states but great powers as well. China's rise and Russia's chauvinistic resurgence do not suggest a high chance of war, but they do underscore the ongoing value of a general, reassuring U.S. military presence in key regions around the world. Even more, extremist states such as Iran and North Korea merit ongoing attention—and ongoing efforts at deterrence. But those who suggest that the United States focus primarily on potential conflict of the traditional sort go too far.[6] Such conflicts are on balance unlikely. Focusing on the remote possibility that they could occur will not be a successful means of holding together key alliances with a forward-looking agenda. In a world of al Qaeda and related movements, as well as numerous weak states vulnerable to collapse or takeover (some with nuclear weapons), the United States cannot afford to direct most of its attentions to classic warfare. Addressing terrorism, civil conflict, reconstruction, and stabilization also matter a great deal, as noted in the third bullet point above.

Homeland security is unlikely to be the main driver for American military forces in the foreseeable future, and the Department of Defense is unlikely to be the lead player in most homeland security missions in any event. As such, the final bullet point noted above will not drive most resource decisions for the Pentagon. That said, clearly there can be no more important objective for any military than directly protecting its own country's territory, so this objective merits inclusion on any short list of U.S. national security goals.

The first two objectives listed above are the main determinants of the U.S. force posture, which, as noted, consists of roughly 1.5 million active duty troops from the four services, plus nearly a million reservists (all backed up by some 700,000 full-time DoD civilian employees and large numbers of contractors). They also require a degree of military modernization that deters would-be competitors from even feeling the temptation to challenge the United States and its chief allies in key overseas theaters.

The final two items above, covering the range of missions from peacekeeping to counterterrorism to homeland defense, have never been the principal determinants of force structure or weapons procurement policy. But they have been important just the same, increasingly so over time. They have greatly affected training and military education in recent years. They have also affected the details of force structure, such as numbers of military police and foreign area officers as well as the Army's modularity plan for restructuring brigades and the Air Force's expeditionary wing concept for organizing forces into smaller deployable packages. The imperative to focus more on homeland defense—as the military's role in homeland security is often described—led to the creation of Northern Command as well as new, specialized units to counter weapons of mass destruction at home or abroad.

Understanding the U.S. Defense Budget

Is the U.S. defense budget inherently high or low? And regardless of one's views on this broad question, what are the more specific budgetary implications of possible defense policy changes?

Starting with the broad question, many who wish to defend the magnitude of Pentagon spending often point out that in recent decades its share of the nation's economy is modest by historical standards. During the 1960s, national defense spending was typically 8 to 9 percent of gross domestic product; in the 1970s it began at around 8 percent and declined to just under 5 percent of GDP; during the Reagan buildup of the 1980s, it reached 6 percent of GDP before declining somewhat as the cold war ended. In the 1990s it started at roughly 5 percent and wound up around 3 percent. During the first term of President George W. Bush, the figure reached 4 percent by 2005 and stayed there through 2007; it grew toward 4.5 percent by 2009. Seen in this light, current levels (including wartime supplemental budgets) seem relatively moderate, if hardly low.[7] Similarly, U.S. defense spending is also now about 20 percent of federal government outlays, in contrast to nearly half in the 1960s, for example.[8]

By contrast, those who criticize the Pentagon budget often note that it constitutes almost half of aggregate global military spending (to be precise, 41 percent in both 2005 and 2006, according to the estimates of the International Institute for Strategic Studies).[9] Or they note that estimated 2009 national security discretionary spending of some $670 billion exceeds the cold war inflation-adjusted spending average of $450 billion (expressed in 2009 dollars, as are most of the below costs unless otherwise noted) by almost 50 percent once war costs are included (and exceeds the cold war average modestly even *without* war costs). Or they note that it dwarfs the size of the United States' diplomatic, foreign assistance, and homeland security spending levels (roughly $13 billion, $25 billion, and $44 billion, respectively, in 2009).[10]

These broad arguments are all simultaneously valid, suggesting that they are not themselves conclusive. My own interpretation is that it is hard to view U.S. defense spending as modest, or the military as chronically underfunded, when examining the aggregate of the above statistics. But it is also hard to declare conclusively that a military asked to do so much in so many parts of the world is blatantly excessive. To make useful policy recommendations, including those aimed at reducing defense spending, we must look deeper, and with more specificity, at different elements of the defense budget.

To help policymakers do so, the U.S. military breaks down its budget several ways. One way shows spending by military service (although Marine Corps budgets are generally merged with those of the Navy, since the Marine Corps is technically part of the Department of the Navy). Many intelligence community costs are found within the Air Force budget when costs are subdivided this way. A second approach categorizes spending by *title,* or the general function to which funds are

TABLE 2-2. Department of Defense Discretionary Budget
Authority, by Title[a]
Billions of constant FY 2009 dollars

Category	2009	2010	2011	2012	2013
Military personnel	125.2	124.7	126.0	126.9	127.3
Operations and maintenance	179.8	177.4	178.8	177.1	179.1
Procurement	104.2	111.1	113.2	115.4	115.6
Research, development, testing, and evaluation	79.6	75.4	69.6	66.9	63.3
Military construction	21.2	17.5	13.9	10.8	9.4
Family housing	3.3	2.6	2.0	1.9	1.7
Revolving and management funds/other	3.5	3.0	2.3	2.7	2.0
Total	516.8	511.7	505.8	501.7	498.5

Source: U.S. Department of Defense, *National Defense Budget Estimates for FY 2009* (Washington, March 2008), p. 60 (www.defenselink.mil/comptroller/defbudget/fy2009/FY09 Greenbook/greenbook_2009_updated.pdf).

a. Totals are for each fiscal year and exclude supplemental appropriations. Totals may not add up because of rounding.

devoted—the way funding is broken down in appropriations bills. (See table 2-2 for the Bush administration's last projections.)

Another method, devised by former secretary of defense Robert McNamara, subdivides spending by what he called military "programs." McNamara sought to be more explicit in the type of actual military activity funded by different pools of funds. These programs include strategic nuclear capabilities, main combat forces, transportation assets, administrative and related support activities, National Guard and reserve forces, and intelligence, as well as several smaller areas of expenditure. This method is itself not perfectly revealing or even accurate. Many military forces are usable for both nuclear and conventional operations, for example, and some equipment is first bought for active duty forces but later transferred to the reserves. Moreover, these categories are sufficiently broad that, even if accurate, they may have only modest bearing on informing a policy choice. But they still give at least an order of magnitude sense of how different types of military objectives or main activities translate into costs.

In federal parlance, the Department of Defense budget plus those parts of the Department of Energy budget that fund nuclear weapons activities are together known as the *national security budget,* or the 050 function in the federal budget. International affairs programs including diplomacy and foreign assistance are labeled as the 150 account; veterans' benefits are found within the 700 function; homeland security is distributed among a range of accounts.

At present, the Department of Energy's share of national security or 050 spending is about $18 billion a year. There is another $6 billion spent here and there by other agencies. But the bulk of the 050 money is of course for the Department of Defense. As for DoD, estimated spending in fiscal year 2009 is as noted roughly $670 billion. Viewed in terms of budget authority, the underlying peacetime budget for 2009 in the Bush administration's request was $515 billion. Another $70 billion was requested as an initial supplemental for the final months of calendar 2008 and beginning of 2009, with more funding expected in the course of 2009. By way of comparison, supplemental budget authority had totaled about $170 billion in 2007 and $195 billion in 2008 (again, these figures are expressed in 2009 dollars).

Cumulatively over the decade, with these initial supplemental appropriations for fiscal year 2009, total costs for Iraq were $657 billion ($621 billion of it was DoD money); for Afghanistan $173 billion ($160 billion of it was DoD money); and for DoD's role in homeland security, $28 billion. The grand total of post-9/11 wartime costs was thus $858 billion, with $809 billion of it for the Department of Defense.[11]

The following tables reflect the Bush administration's request for 2009, only modestly different from what Congress approved, using the three different approaches discussed above (and not counting any war costs). The budget authority figures include about $2.9 billion in so-called mandatory spending but are predominantly discretionary in nature (tables 2-3, 2-4, 2-5).[12]

In the chapters that follow, these budgetary breakdowns help provide context that will be useful in considering defense policy alternatives. For example, they show that, not including wartime supplementals, overall funding for the three military departments is roughly distributed equally (although it should be recalled that the entry for the Navy Department includes the Marine Corps budget, and the Air Force Department includes much of the intelligence budget). They also show that procurement funding has reestablished itself as a large component of the Pentagon

TABLE 2-3. Department of Defense 2009 Budget Authority
Request, by Title

Billions of dollars

Military Personnel	128.9
Operations and Maintenance	180.4
Procurement	104.2
Research, Development, Testing, and Evaluation	79.6
Military Construction and Family Housing	24.4
Management Funds, Transfers, Receipts	0.8
Total	518.3

Source: Office of the Under Secretary of Defense (Comptroller), *Military Personnel Programs (M-1), Operation and Maintenance Programs (O-1), Department of Defense Budget, Fiscal Year 2009* (Department of Defense, February 2008), pp. 18, 20; *Construction Programs (C-1), Department of Defense Budget, Fiscal Year 2009* (Department of Defense, February 2008), p. iv; *Procurement Programs (P-1), Department of Defense Budget, Fiscal Year 2009* (Department of Defense, February 2008), p. II; *RDT&E Programs (R-1), Department of Defense Budget, Fiscal Year 2009* (Department of Defense, February 2008), p. II.

TABLE 2-4. Department of Defense 2009 Budget Authority
Request, by Service

Billions of dollars

Army	139.0
Navy	149.0
Air Force	143.7
DoD-wide	86.6
Total	518.3

Source: Office of the Under Secretary of Defense (Comptroller), Tina W. Jonas, *Fiscal Year 2009 Budget Request: Summary Justification* (Department of Defense, February 4, 2008), p. 8.

budget, after the 1990s in which it diminished quite a bit. Research and development funding is still robust (note that the corresponding entry varies a great deal from one table to the next, since in one case it includes testing and evaluation, whereas in the other case it does not). And DoD's fraction of nuclear weapons spending, not counting missile defense or Department of Energy nuclear costs, is in an intermediate zone. It is far less than it once was, to be sure, but is at roughly $10 billion a year, still real money.

TABLE 2-5. Department of Defense 2009 Budget, by Program (Total Obligational Authority)[a]

Billions of dollars

Strategic Forces	9.9
General Purpose Forces	201.9
Command, Control, Communications, Intelligence, and Space	77.6
Mobility Forces	13.5
Guard and Reserve Forces	38.4
Research and Development	52.8
Central Supply and Maintenance	22.0
Training, Medical, and Other	70.6
Administration	18.8
Support of Other Nations	2.2
Special Operations Forces	9.0
Other	0.1
Total	516.8

Source: See Office of the Under Secretary of Defense (Comptroller), *National Defense Budget Estimates for FY 2008* (Department of Defense), pp. 1–2, 81; Office of Management and Budget, *Budget of the United States Government, Fiscal Year 2008: Historical Tables* (Government Printing Office, 2007), pp. 89, 164; Allen Schick, *The Federal Budget: Politics, Policy, Process* (Brookings, 2007), p. 57.

a. Here the figures add up to a slightly different total because what is presented is total obligational authority, not budget authority. The difference in these two concepts is quite small for our purposes, but it has to do with the possibility that some funds and some obligations can carry over from one year to the next (or lapse or be eliminated before being obligated), creating a slight difference between budget authority and total obligational authority in any given year.

Another detail worth noting here concerns the distinction between discretionary budgets and overall, total budgets. Discretionary funds have to be appropriated each year by Congress. Overall budgets also include mandatory programs and spending—which do not require yearly attention (entitlements are the largest example of mandatory programs in the federal budget). Almost all military spending is discretionary, though not quite all. Mandatory accounts can be positive or negative as they can involve trust funds, user-fee programs, and the like. For example, in 2008 the administration's request for all DoD funding was $643.7 billion; the discretionary request was for $647.2 billion, meaning that the mandatory funding request was "negative."

COMPARISONS OF U.S. DEFENSE SPENDING WITH OTHER COUNTRIES

Most of the above focuses on the U.S. defense budget. This is appropriate. Only by knowing how much various changes to the U.S. military force structure, global posture, or war fighting operations would cost or save can they be properly evaluated and compared with other national priorities within or outside the 050 budget category. But it is also important to understand the Untied States' defense budget in a global context. After all, military capabilities only have meaning in relation to the capabilities of other states or actors. Comparative military spending levels are hardly definitive for measuring relative power or predicting combat outcomes. But budget comparisons are an important and salient gauge of the effort and resources a country puts into its armed forces, if nothing else. While outputs matter more than inputs, the latter are hardly insignificant.

At this moment in history, two broad questions stand out. First, why is U.S. defense spending so high compared with other countries? Second, and somewhat related, how should one interpret the rapid growth in the defense resources of the People's Republic of China (PRC)?

In 2005, according to the most widely available comparative measurement (by the International Institute for Strategic Studies), actual U.S. expenditures totaled $495.3 billion in nominal dollars out of a global total of $1,207.5 billion—or 41 percent of the world's total. The numbers grew in 2006, but the percentage remained the same. The United States' share may have grown further since then, given the high costs of war supplementals.[13] (See table 2-6 for comparative figures on global military spending for 2007.)

Even if higher estimates of spending are used for some other countries, U.S. defense resources dwarf China's military spending of about $135 billion (see below for more on this), or Russia's spending of about $75 billion (these are expressed in 2009 dollars). Most of the next tier of top military spenders are U.S. allies (France and Britain each spent about $60 billion in 2006; Japan, $45 billion; Germany, $42 billion; and Italy, $34 billion). Saudi Arabia and South Korea rounded off the top ten list at $33 billion and $27 billion, respectively, with India next at $25 billion. Then came another slew of U.S. partners and allies including Australia ($19 billion), Brazil ($18 billion), Canada ($17 billion), Spain ($16 billion), Turkey ($13 billion), Israel ($12 billion), the Netherlands ($11 billion), the United Arab Emirates (UAE) ($10 billion), and Taiwan ($9 billion). Again, these numbers are for 2006.

Among major U.S. worries, the lead spenders are Iran ($8 billion), North Korea (about $2 billion to $5 billion, though estimates are difficult to obtain), Venezuela ($3 billion), Cuba ($2 billion), and Syria ($2 billion).[14] All these latter allocations are very modest—as are the working budgets of groups such as al Qaeda and various Iraqi militias (which measure in the tens or hundreds of millions of dollars a year at most).[15]

TABLE 2-6. Global Distribution of Military Spending, 2007

Countries	Defense expenditure[a]	Percentage of global total	Cumulative percentage
United States	552,568	42.7	43
Formal U.S. Allies			
NATO			
Canada	18,491	1.4	44
France	60,662	4.7	49
Germany	42,108	3.3	52
Italy	37,770	2.9	55
Spain	17,495	1.4	56
Turkey	13,643	1.1	57
United Kingdom	63,258	4.9	62
Rest of NATO[b]	57,480	4.4	67
Total NATO (excluding United States)	310,907	24.0	
Total NATO	863,475	66.7	
Rio Pact[c]	38,394	3.0	70
Key Asia-Pacific Allies			
Japan	41,039	3.2	73
South Korea	26,588	2.1	75
Australia	20,216	1.6	76
New Zealand	1,388	0.1	77
Thailand	3,333	0.3	77
Philippines	1,130	0.1	77
Total Key Asia-Pacific Allies	93,694	7.2	
Informal U.S. Allies			
Israel	11,607	0.9	78
Egypt	4,640	0.4	78
Iraq[d]	9,000	0.7	79
Pakistan	4,530	0.4	79
Gulf Cooperation Council (GCC)[e]	54,160	4.2	83
Jordan	1,621	0.1	84
Morocco	2,409	0.2	84
Mexico	3,982	0.3	84
Taiwan	9,585	0.7	85
Total Informal Allies	101,534	7.8	
Other Nations			
Non-NATO Europe	25,559	2.0	87
Other Middle East and North Africa[f]	7,056	0.5	87

Countries	Defense expenditure[a]	Percentage of global total	Cumulative percentage
Other Nations (continued)			
Other Central and South Asia[g]	3,949	0.3	88
Other East Asia and Pacific[h]	15,363	1.2	89
Other Caribbean and Latin America[i]	181	0.0	89
Sub-Saharan Africa	11,495	0.9	90
Total Other Nations	63,603	4.9	
Major Neutral Nations			
China	46,174	3.6	93
Russia	32,215	2.5	96
India	26,513	2.0	98
Indonesia	4,329	0.3	98
Total Major Neutral Nations	109,231	8.4	
Nemeses and Adversaries			
Iran	7,451	0.6	99
North Korea[d]	2,000–5,000	0.3	99
Syria	1,465	0.1	99
Myanmar	7,009	0.5	100
Venezuela	2,795	0.2	100
Cuba[j]	1,668	0.1	100
Total Nemeses and Adversaries	23,888	1.8	
Total	1,293,819	100.0	

Source: International Institute for Strategic Studies, *The Military Balance 2009* (New York: Routledge Press, 2009), pp. 447–52.

a. Amounts are in current US dollars, in millions.

b. Belgium, Bulgaria, Czech Republic, Denmark, Estonia, Greece, Hungary, Iceland, Latvia, Lithuania, Luxembourg, Netherlands, Norway, Poland, Portugal, Romania, Slovakia. and Slovenia.

c. Argentina, Bahamas, Bolivia, Brazil, Chile, Colombia, Costa Rica, Dominican Republic, Ecuador, El Salvador, Guatemala, Haiti, Honduras, Nicaragua, Panama, Paraguay, Peru, Trinidad and Tobago, and Uruguay. Cuba and Venezuela are also signatories but are not included here to prevent double counting.

d. Data for Iraq and North Korea based on author's estimates.

e. Bahrain, Kuwait, Oman, Qatar, Saudi Arabia. and United Arab Emirates.

f. Algeria, Lebanon, Libya, Mauritania, Tunisia, and Yemen.

g. Afghanistan, Bangladesh, Kazakhstan, Kyrgyzstan, Maldives, Nepal, Sri Lanka, Tajikistan, Turkmenistan, and Uzbekistan.

h. Brunei, Cambodia, Fiji, Laos, Malaysia, Mongolia, Papua New Guinea, Singapore, Timor Leste, and Vietnam.

i. Antigua and Barbuda, Barbados, Belize, Jamaica, and Suriname.

j. Data for 2007 are not available for Cuba; 2006 data are shown.

For some, the information above is enough to conclude that U.S. defense spending is not only large but exorbitant and unnecessary—especially in an era of large U.S. budget and trade deficits. Indeed, when NATO and east Asian allies are figured in, the western alliance system accounts for about 75 percent of global military spending; when other allies in places such as South America are also included, and countries having security partnerships with the United States such as Taiwan and Israel and the Persian Gulf sheikdoms are tallied too, the broader U.S.-led global alliance system's military spending reaches 85 percent of the world's total.

An important reason for the United States' high defense spending is its large number of overseas interests and allies. Allies add to the strength of the western alliance on what might be called the supply side, but they also potentially add burdens on the United States on the demand side. With several dozen formal security partners, and large military deployments in three main regions of the world (east Asia, Europe, and the broader Middle East) as well as smaller commitments in numerous other places, the United States has many actual and potential military obligations. Moreover, these distant theaters all require substantial effort to reach for U.S. forces, adding to the difficulty of the potential missions—and limiting the utility of comparative defense budget analysis, since potential enemies would generally be fighting on or near their home turf.

Another important explanation for the disproportionately large U.S. defense budget is that the United States seeks a major qualitative advantage in military capability. It is not interested in a fair fight, that is to say an even competition. Rather, it seeks a major military advantage. Such superiority, so the logic goes, should enhance deterrence by reducing the likelihood that other countries will choose to challenge the U.S. military. To put it more negatively, history is full of examples in which the smaller military, and quite often the less expensive one, prevails in battle against a larger and nominally stronger foe. So modest advantages may not be adequate. While high spending cannot totally overcome the distinct possibility that the underdog will win in war, it can certainly make the underdog's job much harder.

Qualitative superiority also helps compensate for the modest size of the U.S. armed forces, which have been severely strained in the process of trying to stabilize two mid-sized nations of about 25 million people each in recent years. The active duty U.S. military, at about 1.4 million uniformed personnel, is certainly not large in a historical or a current international perspective. Not only is it down from the range of 2.0 to 2.25 million that characterized the post-Vietnam, cold war military (and down from much higher levels during the Vietnam and Korea wars), it represents less than 10 percent of the world's total of more than 20 million individuals under arms. China leads the way at 2.1 million. India at 1.3 million, North Korea at 1.1 million, and Russia at 1.0 million are not too far behind the United States by this measure. (South Korea, Pakistan, Iran, Turkey, Egypt, and Vietnam occupy the next tier in terms of size, with armed forces ranging from 450,000 to 700,000 personnel each.)[16]

The mention of China, moreover, underscores the point that U.S. defense planning must look to the future, not just the present. A country with 2.1 million persons under arms, a military spending level probably exceeding $100 billion a year and growing fast, and irredentist claims on a key U.S. economic and security partner (Taiwan) demands at least some concern. Yet, it is also important to place this spending in perspective and not be more worried about it than the evidence would warrant. (It is also important to recognize the extreme economic interdependence of these two countries, with China financing so much of the U.S. budget deficit in recent years and the United States providing so much of the market for Chinese goods. It is to be hoped that these mutual dependencies further reduce the risk of war.)

The People's Republic of China's official defense budget at market exchange rates was $46 billion in 2007. But that figure is just the starting point for gauging China's military resource allocations.

There are two main reasons why the PRC official number substantially understates actual military resources. First, because of limited transparency in its official papers and budgets, it fails to include many defense activities commonly recognized as intrinsic to a military budget by standard NATO definitions (or common sense). These feature foreign arms purchases, military-related research and development, nuclear weapons activities, and paramilitary forces. Altogether, the absence of these categories of expenditure creates a significant error in the official budget. Thankfully, corrections can be made with reasonable accuracy. For example, China's arms purchases from abroad (largely from Russia) in recent years have reached roughly the $2 billion to $3 billion annual level, and its nuclear costs are probably in a roughly comparable range, as are its research and development costs. Various types of industrial subsidies given to its defense industry may total $5 billion to $10 billion a year. Overall, when adjustments are made to the official budget to account for such undercounting, the total budget probably increases $15 billion to $20 billion a year.[17]

Second, as a developing economy, China (like many other countries) has a number of military-related costs that are quite inexpensive by Western standards. When China's defense budget is expressed in dollars, therefore, and a comparative sense of its military resource allocation is sought, it is more useful to express figures in terms of purchasing power parity than straight exchange-rate comparisons. Making such conversions is difficult. For example, the fact that a Chinese soldier can be fed and housed much more cheaply than a Western soldier is an advantage for the PRC, and should probably be acknowledged in any careful comparison, the fact that a typical Western soldier's education and salary are much more expensive reflects a qualitative advantage of that soldier. So not all costs can be converted the same way.[18]

When all is said and done, the United States government has typically estimated China's actual military resource levels as two to three times its official numbers. A reasonable midpoint estimate for China's spending level in 2006 is thus about $135 billion, and the 2007 level may have reached close to $150 billion.[19]

As noted, this only provides general context. For a possible conflict, say over Taiwan, would China's greater geographic proximity and greater sense of national vital interest allow it to fight the United States to a draw—or at least have a chance to do so—in any future war? It is hard to determine the answer from defense budget comparisons alone. The point here is simply to establish some sense of the scale of China's effort and the pace at which it is accelerating that effort.

The main message of the above can be summarized as follows. U.S. military spending is indeed very high. There is no serious way to argue otherwise. Yet its burden on the U.S. economy, even in these difficult times, is substantially less than it was during most of the cold war, and the advantage it confers on the United States vis-à-vis other countries is not something to regret or to discard. Moreover, the sheer number of U.S. strategic commitments around the world necessitates a robustly funded Department of Defense. The benefits of this well-resourced military to not just the United States but the international community in general are substantial. That said, the Pentagon can and should look for belt-tightening measures—especially given the need to expand support for underfinanced national security needs in other, nonmilitary realms. Given the nature of today's challenges, with stabilization missions being so important as antidotes to terrorism, global crime, drug production, the spread of infectious disease, and other real threats to U.S. well being, nonmilitary instruments for conducting such missions have also become central to U.S. national security.[20] The underlying philosophy should be one of economizing where possible in military spending, in part to facilitate modest increases in these other tools of national security—but not of risking the excellence that U.S. military forces display on the international stage.

THE CURRENT STATE OF THE U.S. MILITARY

For all the resources pumped into it, the U.S. military is still under severe strain. As noted above, it is not particularly large given all the burdens placed upon it, particularly by ongoing wars in Iraq and Afghanistan. Some contend that the U.S. armed forces are at or near a breaking point. If true, this would be of momentous concern, overriding traditional resource allocation decisions about how many fighter jets or surface combatants or attack submarines to buy and field and necessitating urgent consideration of a radical reduction in America's military commitments abroad. Indeed, President Obama has indicated concerns along these lines, and his campaign plan for rapid withdrawal from Iraq was premised partly on the need to alleviate the strain on the ground forces. Whether things are in desperate straits or not, it is important to get as precise a feel as possible for the strain on the military when considering future policy options for Iraq and Afghanistan—not to mention Darfur and the Congo (Democratic Republic of the Congo). As such, a review of the state of U.S. military readiness is in order. Thankfully, the data suggest that the situation is not as dire as some argue—though strains are admittedly real and limit future options on force allocations and probably place a ceiling on aggregate overseas deployments at roughly the current level for the foreseeable future.

Secretary Gates has argued that the United States faces no urgent readiness crisis. That is to say, its forces continue to perform impressively on the battlefields of Iraq and Afghanistan, suggesting that they are tolerating current strain reasonably well even at great individual sacrifice. (This is not to say that the Afghanistan war, as of this writing in early 2009, is going well. In fact, it is not, and the planned doubling of U.S. resources there is necessary in an effort to reverse the slide. Rather, my point is that the performance of individual units in the missions they are being asked to carry out remains generally quite good.) And its residual airpower and naval power constitute potent deterrents against possible aggression or conflict in Korea, the Persian Gulf, or the Taiwan Strait.[21]

But what do the data say about whether today's U.S. military is nearing the point of extreme wear, tear, and exhaustion? If it were, the consequences could be even more severe than the possibility of failing to achieve the nation's core goals in Iraq and Afghanistan. The greatest worry, to be specific, is that the military could enter into a vicious cycle whereby soldiers and marines (in particular) start leaving the force in droves because of excessive deployments, leaving a smaller number of people to do the same missions, which in turn leads to even greater exhaustion—and attrition—among those who initially stay. If the process develops a certain momentum, traditional policy tools may be unable to compensate, and the very integrity of the all-volunteer military could then be put at risk.

Readiness has often been a political football. In the 1970s, America's military was alleged—in that case, largely correctly—to have gone hollow. A substantial force structure existed, but it was not particularly strong within, and it did not hold up very well when called upon to perform. During the mid to late 1990s, similar allegations about the U.S. military were made as the armed forces were downsized in the aftermath of the cold war.[22] In the first decade of the twenty-first century, as the Iraq and Afghanistan missions have continued relentlessly, many have spoken of a U.S. Army that has become broken.

What are these criticisms about? What do terms like *hollow* and *broken* even mean in the context of military preparedness? And what does the United States need to do to ensure its military will remain strong after the trials, tribulations, and stresses of the Iraq and Afghanistan wars— which have been tremendous learning and toughening experiences for the military at one level but extraordinarily difficult at another? In fact, today's military readiness metrics using official Pentagon data do reveal considerably more strain, and more gaps in preparedness relative to desired standards, than was seen, for example, in the 1990s. (It should be added that the Pentagon has been less forthcoming with readiness data in recent years, so this judgment is based on incomplete information.) Thankfully, it is clear that the problems are much less severe than they were in the 1970s and 1960s. Such sweeping assessments of readiness are insufficient, however; we must look deeper and more specifically at various aspects of readiness.

Evaluation of readiness is simplest if we begin by dividing the subject into three broad categories: personnel, training, and equipment. Unfortunately, during the Rumsfeld era, the Pentagon became more secretive, and much of the information previously available was held more closely. But we can still evaluate some trends, placing them in historical context to get a sense of the severity of today's concerns.

PERSONNEL

Consider several trends in U.S. military personnel that arose during the George W. Bush administration. The military has accepted more recruits with general equivalency degrees rather than high school diplomas; it has enlisted a higher percentage of applicants scoring very low on its aptitude tests; and it has also taken on more individuals over forty years old as first-time military personnel.

The trend lines on age and general equivalency diplomas (GEDs) began to cause concern in the last few years. The GED is considered academically equivalent to a high school diploma, and the military can ensure that anyone with such qualifications is up to par by testing them in other ways too, but it is still not seen as the degree of choice. While figures for the other services have remained good, the Army has experienced some problems. Its high school graduation figure for new recruits for 2005 dipped to about 80 percent (worse than the 1985 figure of 86 percent, though still much better than the typical level of about 55 percent of the 1970s).[23] By 2007, the percentage of high school graduates had declined to below 80 percent.[24] Thankfully, the situation improved in 2008, with figures exceeding 80 percent, as tougher economic conditions combined with improved battlefield trends helped recruiting.[25] And 2008 was the third straight year that the active duty Army met its recruiting goals—admittedly in part because of a worsened general economy on the one hand, and more bonuses and recruitment waivers on matters such as criminal record on the other.[26]

There has been a recent rumor that West Point graduates have been leaving the service at drastically increased rates as soon as their minimal obligations are satisfied. In fact, this appears not to be true. The last year for which data are available as of this writing (the class of 2002, which was eligible to leave the service as of 2007) showed a 68 percent reenlistment rate, only 4 percentage points below the 1990s average.[27] More generally, company grade officers (first and second lieutenants as well as captains) have not been leaving the force at a greater than normal rate either; the average rate during the Iraq war has been less than the average rate of the late 1990s, for example.[28] A similar conclusion is true of majors.[29] Nonetheless, the Army is now short several thousand officers in aggregate.[30] This is largely because the Army is increasing the number of officers needed as it enlarges the number of brigades in its force structure. In addition, the Army did not enlist enough young officers in the early 1990s, meaning that the current pool of officers from which to recruit for mid-level positions is too small.[31]

Other matters are more worrisome. While the number of individuals scoring relatively high on aptitude tests remains better than in the 1980s, trends are in the wrong direction.[32] Moral waivers for matters such as criminal history have increased substantially in recent years, with a total of 860 soldiers and marines requiring waivers from convictions for felony crimes in 2007, up by 400 just from the year 2006. While most of the convictions were for juvenile theft, and the aggregate total is modest compared with the size of the force, only by arresting such trends will the quality of the force be ensured.[33]

Divorce rates have leveled off somewhat at about 3.5 percent a year, after reaching 3.9 percent in 2004, and are not worse than in the general population—but they are still above the 2.9 percent level of 2003.[34]

Suicide rates are a significant problem for the military, and of course an extremely tragic reality for so many troops and their families. The rate reached 17.3 per 100,000 soldiers in the U.S. Army in 2006. That was not far off from the age-adjusted and gender-adjusted average for the U.S. population on the whole (for males, for example, the rate is 17.6 per 100,000). But the rate continued to grow, reaching 20.2 per 100,000 in 2008—the first time since Vietnam when rates within the military exceeded those outside.[35] They are also now much higher than the rate of 9.1 per 100,000 soldiers in 2001 and as such are a serious reason for worry.[36]

For one group of soldiers surveyed in 2008, among those who had been to Iraq on three or four separate tours, the fraction displaying signs of post-traumatic stress disorders was 27 percent (in contrast to 12 percent after one tour and 18.5 percent after two). As of early 2008, among the 513,000 active duty soldiers who have served in Iraq, more than 197,000 had served more than once, and more than 53,000 had deployed three or more times.[37]

If an overall assessment was to be offered of the U.S. ground forces today, it is that of an Army and Marine Corps under serious strain but collectively holding up. Most indicators are not worsening, although they are less healthy than in most periods of the 1980s and 1990s. As such, complacency is hardly in order; we should be concerned that the reasonably good readiness of the military today is fragile and not sustainable indefinitely. Moreover, at the individual level, many soldiers and marines are facing enormous hardship, raising fairness and equity issues for a democracy that is asking so few to do so much for so long on behalf of the nation.[38] As such, several policy initiatives are considered below in an effort to help some of those suffering the most strain today.

TRAINING

In most of the Vietnam era, military training was not nearly rigorous enough. But great attention was focused on this matter in the 1970s and 1980s, demanding regimens were developed, resources were amply provided for training, and subsequent military performance was seen to improve greatly. This was validated not only in training but in military operations such as the 1986 air attack on Libya, the invasion of Panama, and eventually Operation Desert Storm. Ever since that period, Reagan-era standards have remained important in determining how forces should be prepared—from basic training to specialized training to unit training at main bases to large-formation training at the various weapons schools and combat training centers.

As with personnel, today's most important training issue concerns the ground forces. Soldiers and marines have virtually no time to do anything more than deploy to the theater of combat, return, rest, and then prepare to go back. Generalized training in other types of combat, besides the counterinsurgency and counterterrorism now being carried out in Iraq and Afghanistan, is by necessity being neglected. The assumption is that forces who performed so brilliantly in classic combat in 2003, and who have been so hardened by ongoing combat of a different type since then, will remain proficient for the full range of possible missions for the foreseeable future even without the full range of training as required by official doctrine. But that is an assumption, not an obvious truth. The assumption can be periodically tested by asking modest numbers of troops to be subjected to tough assessments of their skills in other types of combat on the training ranges (even if there is not enough time or there are not enough resources to do so for most formations). But again, there is a level of uncertainty with measuring readiness that is hard to eliminate entirely.

For the moment, there is little choice in the matter. The nation must do what it can to prevail in Iraq and Afghanistan, and the importance of those real wars trumps the hypothetical significance of possible but unlikely wars elsewhere that can, in any case, often be largely addressed through naval and air capabilities. In fact, recent efforts have been aimed at further improving preparation for the missions we are involved in today, through improved coordination across agencies and other such refinements of training and operations (as reflected, for example, in the recent promulgation of the State and Defense "COIN Handbook for Policymakers," or "U.S. Government Counterinsurgency Guide," released in January 2009). Over time, however, the ground forces will need to consider how to balance their development of different skills—a problem discussed further below.

EQUIPMENT

Assessing equipment readiness is in the end probably easier than doing so for people or even training. It is generally a question of countable hardware, not human skills. The hard part is figuring out the broader significance of specific shortfalls in a modest number of equipment categories.

Sometimes a shortfall in one area can be balanced out by surpluses elsewhere. Consider the state of the U.S. Army in recent years. For most major types of vehicles—all classes of helicopters, Abrams tanks and Bradley fighting vehicles, medium-weight trucks—there has been no major crisis due to the wars in Iraq and Afghanistan. No more than 20 percent of the total inventory of most weapons has been in the Central Command theater at a time (according to a 2007 Congressional Budget Office study by Frances Lussier). For most major fighting vehicles and helicopters, there was no shortage of usable equipment for forces based back in the United States, even when equipment in depot or otherwise in disrepair is also accounted for. There *were,* however, notable shortfalls of new types of equipment not yet fielded in abundance—up-armored High Mobility Multipurpose Wheeled Vehicles (HMMWVs), mine-resistant–ambush-protected vehicles (or MRAPS), Strykers—as well as two of seven types of trucks. For the trucks, since there were substantial surpluses in some of the other five categories of trucks, this shortage probably posed little major problem. For the other vehicles, however, there would clearly be great difficulty in finding a way to deploy many to any new scenario that might develop fast. So the Army equipment readiness issue is quite specific—potentially significant for some scenarios, much less so for others. On balance, while Iraq and Afghanistan have taxed the equipment inventories of the U.S. ground forces in particular, the far greater strain at this point is on people, not weaponry.[39]

TOWARD A MORE EFFICIENT MILITARY

With the above as backdrop, the book now turns to laying out a vision for future American defense policy and for budget priorities.

The above discussion of international comparisons of defense spending may lead some to assume that the United States, which accounts for more than 40 percent of the world's military spending (and is formally or informally allied with countries that together account for more than half the remainder), should be able to cut its defense budget substantially. A similar argument might be made by those comparing today's inflation-adjusted military budget to those of the cold war and noting that today's base budget exceeds the cold war average while overall defense spending (including war costs from Iraq and Afghanistan) roughly equals the cold war peak.

However, those making such arguments rarely say how far the cuts could and should go, on the basis of their methodologies. In fact, we cannot build a military out of cold war era people, so the historical comparisons only go so far. (Most military costs go up substantially faster than inflation, since equipment incorporates new and expensive technology; military health care experiences the same general upward pressure on costs felt throughout society; personnel costs tend to rise faster than inflation as we seek to maintain a high-quality, all-volunteer military in time of war; and so on. So even these real-dollar comparisons have limited utility.) And if it is excessive that we outspend China 4 to 1 and Iran nearly 100 to 1, what ratios are appropriate, and why? 2 to 1? 1 to 1?

In fact, such broad contrasts only go so far. Similar problems result when some hawks try to argue, motivated by the opposite goal of increasing defense spending, that we should be willing to spend nearly as high a percentage of our GDP on defense as we did in the latter cold war decades. The cold war era was a different world. Why should it be a useful guide in any way to current policy?

In fact, this book is premised on the notion that, in fact, defense spending needs to be based on examinations of likely threats and missions as well as projected future needs for the U.S. military, and force posture as well as defense budgets then need to be built up from those conceptual foundations. It also proceeds from the assumption that current policy is not a bad starting point, so proposed changes can be made relative to that benchmark.

Turning away from generalities, then, and to specifics, where do we stand in making U.S. defense policy? On the one hand, it has been serving the nation well, preserving a level of great power, peace, and global stability, allowing an impressive period of global economic growth that began shortly after World War II. But Iraq, and before that Afghanistan, has proved two other things about today's U.S. military: it is extremely adaptive to new challenges, and it is also generally not optimized for those challenges. While many improvements have been made in the armed forces' capacities for counterterrorism, counterinsurgency, and stabilization missions, many problems remain. Moreover, for those parts of the military that have not been as directly challenged in recent operations, less learning has likely occurred—and therefore more major changes are likely still needed.

Many of the capabilities that the military needs will cost additional money. Alas, money is tight, and most Americans expect the reduction in coming defense supplementals to translate into reduced deficits (or increased domestic spending or reduced taxes), rather than new military programs. As such, the proposals offered here are intended to be economical relative to the range of possible measures that could be envisioned to address certain needs. And they are accompanied by proposals for belt-tightening in many other existing programs. These programs are generally worthwhile, but as government budgeting is always a process of squaring ends with means—and establishing priorities among competing worthwhile ideas—it is appropriate to ask where most of a given program's benefits can be achieved at lower cost.

It is worth noting that, while the Department of Defense certainly wastes a great deal of money, identifying the waste is rarely easy. Competition, outsourcing, and use of best business practices can produce savings but generally in the range of hundreds of millions of dollars a year, not more.[40] Other reductions in Pentagon spending will generally necessitate tough decisions about which capabilities can be done without in the future.

The next two chapters discuss a number of new and needed initiatives for improving future U.S. defense capabilities:

—A dedicated National Guard brigade for homeland defense and disaster response

—Improved "high demand–low density" assets in the nation's ground forces (especially foreign area officers, military police, and other key capabilities)

—A "peace operations division" within the active Army

—Accelerated Nunn-Lugar programs and related efforts for nuclear security (focused on research reactors around the world)

—Enhanced unmanned aeriel vehicle (UAV) and robotics programs

—Enhanced training and equipping programs for African and other foreign militaries

To pay for these initiatives, while also ensuring adequate funds for non-DoD parts of the nation's security agenda and maintaining fiscal discipline as well, the chapters also advocate economies in a number of areas:

—Nuclear forces

—Some elements of missile defenses

—Future Combat System, or FCS, vehicles (but not sensors, robotics, or communications)

—Advanced combat aircraft

—Submarines, with more based on Guam, but fewer overall in the force structure, and more dual-crewing of other ships

These ideas are numerous enough that it is helpful to break them into two broad groups, which I define as nuclear and conventional. The terminology is somewhat traditionalist, in that there is considerable blurring of lines across these categories. But while the breakdown is imperfect in this regard, it is probably the simplest and most natural that could be employed in this way.

CHAPTER THREE

NUCLEAR WEAPONS
AND MISSILE DEFENSES

NUCLEAR WEAPONS ARE NO longer a dominant aspect of the United States' national security budget, as they were during the cold war when annual costs routinely were well in excess of $50 billion a year. But their budgetary significance is hardly trivial, especially when the Department of Defense as well as relevant parts of the Department of Energy that build and maintain nuclear weapons are considered together. Meanwhile, missile defenses are more important, and more costly, than ever. And all of these subjects are at the heart of many contemporary defense policy debates as well.[1] (See figure 3-1.)

Nuclear deterrence remains important for the United States and its allies. Recognizing that it is highly unlikely that weapons will ever be used, the United States' arsenal nonetheless creates a certain psychological calming effect in countries that may be near Russia, China, North Korea, or another nuclear power. It constitutes a possible answer to extreme biological agents that may be developed in the future as well. That said, nuclear weapons also represent a huge latent danger to the planet, motivating the recent movement that attempts to abolish them across the globe, as discussed below. So the trick is how to reduce them without so upsetting key U.S. allies that nuclear proliferation is accelerated rather than discouraged. It is this logic that motivates my suggestion

FIGURE 3-1. Historical Funding for the Missile Defense Agency and Its Predecessors[a]

Billions of 2009 dollars

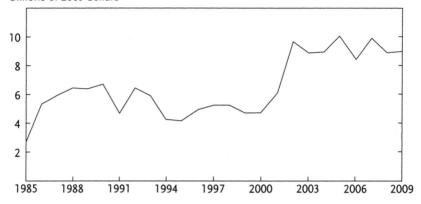

Source: Department of Defense, Missile Defense Agency, "Historical Funding for MDA FY85–09" table (www.mda.mil/mdaLink/pdf/histfunds.pdf [April 16, 2009]).

a. Historical funding levels are for the Strategic Defense Initiative Organization (SDIO), the Ballistic Missile Defense Organization (BMDO), and the Missile Defense Agency (MDA). SDIO was the predecessor to the MDA. Amounts are in constant FY 2009 dollars.

for aiming at a strategic arsenal of 1,000 warheads each for the United States and Russia. That level seems sufficient to provide theoretical military options against nonurban targets that make deterrence at least somewhat credible and to remain superior to that of any third party so as to discourage medium powers from seeking nuclear parity with Washington and Moscow—yet also meaningfully enough reduced to give significant impetus to disarmament efforts.

DRAMATICALLY REDUCING NUCLEAR WEAPONS

In recent years, a movement has begun to advocate the complete and verifiable elimination of nuclear weapons from the face of the Earth. When running for president, Barack Obama endorsed this movement, and key national security experts including Sam Nunn, Bill Perry, George Schultz, and Henry Kissinger have done so as well.

A treaty imposing such a sweeping and historic change in nuclear weaponry is a long ways off, even in the eyes of its most enthusiastic supporters. Technologies do not yet exist to find nuclear materials well hidden by those who would seek to violate any such treaty. And many key countries around the world with nuclear weapons, not just the United States, are far from being willing to give them up. But according to treaty proponents, only by announcing and pursuing such a goal can pressure be maintained on countries like Iran and North Korea, which justify their nuclear ambitions with the complaint that it is discriminatory for the world to allow major powers to keep the bomb while others are deprived.

The notion of nuclear abolition is a complex one. It does have advantages. But at a time when many countries in the Middle East and East Asia are nervous about proliferant behavior by their neighbors, a U.S. commitment to eliminate the very nuclear deterrent that many U.S. allies count on to counter arsenals by aggressive neighbors could also have major downsides. In fact, it could wind up encouraging the very proliferation it is intended to discourage, if not presented and pursued very carefully.

This is not the place to attempt a bottom-line verdict on the nuclear abolition movement. However, there is clear value in the United States continuing to honor its commitments under the Nuclear Non-Proliferation Treaty (NPT) to minimize its dependence on nuclear forces in its security policy. And given the huge cold war arsenals it built up, considerable fractions of which remain today, there is ample room to move further in the general direction of abolition without jeopardizing the core elements of nuclear deterrence.

Along these lines, the following type of alternative nuclear posture totaling 1,000 U.S. warheads should be considered. It should be backed up by a flexible nuclear posture review, which is in fact already under way this year. That review should benefit from substantial White House input rather than domination by the Pentagon.[2] (Because safe command and control of nuclear forces is obviously an imperative, the nuclear review is also a good place to examine cybersecurity, a growing concern without a natural DoD home as of yet, though the Air Force is poised to create the "24th Air Force" under Air Force Space Command as one part of a clearer bureaucratic focus on these key issues.[3]) It would be easiest to move to such an accord in bilateral negotiations with Russia—though the world's medium nuclear powers, including most notably China, could help by pledging not to expand their arsenals as the traditional two nuclear superpowers continue to downsize theirs. Going to 1,000 warheads would not, however, require formal arms control with the medium powers since it would leave the United States and Russia as the world's two nuclear superpowers even after all reductions were complete (any successive rounds of arms control would, however, be more complicated). Ideally, such a ceiling would include all nuclear warheads. However, Russia might not be enthusiastic about such a sweeping accord, in which case more modest (and perhaps even informal) limits on tactical and surplus warheads could be considered. They would permit most of the savings outlined below still to be realized.[4]

An arsenal of 1,000 total warheads would have considerable flexibility. It would start to move the two nuclear superpowers away from their nuclear war plans and counterforce doctrines of the cold war, to be sure. But it would allow options besides a "city-busting" targeting strategy. It would provide a credible means of attacking conventional force concentrations or major transportation infrastructure, for example—to the extent that was seen as still necessary for deterrence purposes.

Reducing to 1,000 would represent a fivefold cut in strategic nuclear inventories relative to current levels and more than a halving of forces envisioned under the 2002 Moscow Treaty. (Since today's total U.S. nuclear warhead inventory is estimated at around 10,000 all told, with similar if not greater numbers in Russia, a comprehensive ceiling of 1,000 total warheads would represent a tenfold cut if short-range as well as surplus weapons were included.) That Moscow accord, also known as the Strategic Offensive Reduction Treaty (or SORT), requires that deployed offensive forces total no more than 1,700 to 2,200 warheads by 2012. But it is binding only at that time, not before or after (since it expires in 2012), and does not cover nondeployed or tactical warheads either.[5]

Ideally, under any new accord, warheads would be removed from forward locations—to improve safety and to send a message about the more limited role for nuclear weapons in defense postures and strategies. For example, the 200 or so U.S. nuclear weapons still in Europe would be brought back home (and likely destroyed) under this concept.[6] Indeed, bringing the warheads home need not await a treaty.

My proposal for a U.S. nuclear force posture under such a 1,000 warhead accord preserves the so-called triad, including land-based missiles and bombers. Some advocate greater, if not complete, reliance on the submarine force after any such deep cuts. However, submarines are only survivable when at sea, and keeping them at sea with their warheads aboard runs counter to the vision of "de-alerting" nuclear forces so that they are not on hair trigger as they were during the cold war. Although some notions have been advanced for keeping submarines at sea without their warheads, and finding a way to allow them to take on their warheads without returning to port and making themselves vulnerable, such schemes are very complex. So my recommended alternative force posture would feature a mix of capabilities:

—Six Trident submarines each with 100 warheads aboard (down from fourteen submarines today, each with 24 Trident II or D5 missiles, with a grand total of some 2,000 warheads among them, with nine normally focused on the Pacific and five on the Atlantic): the six would operate just as is done today, out of one port on the East Coast and one on the West Coast. A total of two submarines could be at sea at a time to preserve the arsenal's survivability.

—one hundred land-based, single-warhead Minuteman III missiles in hardened silos in the Midwest (down from 450 today, with a total of 1,200 warheads): a certain number of conventionally armed missiles might be exempted from caps, up to a maximum number of perhaps several dozen, if that proved negotiable.[7]

—three hundred warheads deliverable by B-52 or B-2 bomber, with three to four bases in the United States equipped to handle the warheads and thirty planes capable of delivering them: presently there are just over seventy bombers devoted to the nuclear mission, each capable of carrying sixteen to twenty warheads, with twenty B-2 and some fifty-six B-52 available for such purposes.[8]

A treaty with Russia allowing 1,000 warheads per country might also attempt to deal with missile defenses. The best approach would involve sharing of information on planned systems, especially those in the Czech Republic and Poland, if and when they are someday built, together with efforts to collaborate so that defenses would protect Russian as well as U.S.-NATO interests and involve the technologies and assets of both sides. This would be the ideal solution.[9]

But it may not be achievable. In that event, to the extent that U.S. deployment of such defenses was fundamentally a source of antagonism for Russia, and perhaps China, it could be agreed that highly capable systems demonstrated to be effective against ballistic missile threats on test ranges be counted against total caps. In other words, a new treaty could combine offensive and defensive limitations. But any such concept should not treat the two types of weapons in parallel fashion. Offensive nuclear warheads are capable of incinerating cities; defenses are capable only of defeating offensive warheads (since defensive systems are no longer nuclear-tipped). Moreover, given the imperfections of technology, it is generally recognized that more than one defense system or warhead would typically be needed to defeat a notional offensive warhead on average. As such, counting rules might count three to five defensive systems with medium to long range as the equivalent of one offensive system.

The savings from this option over the next decade would be principally in areas of operations and support, since plans for modernizing the offensive nuclear force are modest. The military is currently maintaining and when necessary refurbishing Minuteman missiles and Trident submarine-based capabilities, not pursuing replacement systems. Some of these modification efforts would of course be scaled back under a smaller force posture. But the main savings would arise from reducing intercontinental ballistic missiles (ICBMs) by up to 350 missiles and submarines by up to eight vessels, as well as stopping production of D5 missiles a few years earlier than now planned (the program is currently scheduled to go through 2013). No savings are assumed for the bomber fleet, given its dual-purpose roles; conventional missions would give reason to sustain the force structure even in light of nuclear cutbacks. The ICBMs cost about $2.5 million each per year to operate, the submarines about $70 million each, making for total savings of about $1.5 billion a year if this option can be implemented.[10]

Secretary Gates's proposal to cancel the transformational communications satellite program would also appear to have merit. It is difficult to evaluate thoroughly on the basis of unclassified information, but it appears the program is proving technologically challenging and more expensive than foreseen. While this is hardly just a strategic nuclear capability, it still merits a word here. Its cancellation might ultimately save half the $26 billion program cost if replaced with something less expensive (and also somewhat less capable).[11]

Some cuts could occur even absent a negotiated accord. For example, submarine fleets might be cut back while keeping maximum warhead loadings for now—producing operating savings without making unilateral force cutbacks that some might see as reducing U.S. negotiating leverage with Moscow for an actual treaty. ICBMs might be reduced with more of the total nuclear inventory being placed in the bomber leg of the triad, until a formal treaty was concluded. Surplus and tactical warheads could also be eliminated in substantial numbers, on top of the cuts already made.

NUCLEAR TESTING AND NUCLEAR WARHEAD STEWARDSHIP

The above discussion focuses on the role of the Department of Defense in the nuclear weapons posture, with a focus on the major combat systems carrying the warheads. But the warheads themselves are naturally a huge part of the overall business, and they are primarily the responsibility of the Department of Energy.

Two main considerations determine the cost of the country's nuclear arsenal. The first is its size, as discussed above. The second is its composition, in terms of types of warheads and their underlying purposes. Beyond force structure issues, the central issue with the nuclear warhead inventory is the degree to which it may be modernized in the future—which raises questions of nuclear testing and stockpile stewardship. Maintaining a capacity to develop new weapons, and test new as well as existing weapons, accounts for much of the DoE's nuclear-related costs and is therefore of considerable importance for this study. Adopting a smaller arsenal that does not require ongoing testing, as advocated here, could lead to a substantial scaling back of at least one of DoE's three main weapons labs and eliminate the need to build a new plutonium pit production facility (since the small existing plant at Los Alamos could then suffice). It would also allow ratification of the Comprehensive Test Ban Treaty (CTBT), signed by President Clinton but voted down by the Senate when it considered ratification in the late 1990s. U.S. approval of this treaty could have the additional virtue of promoting nuclear nonproliferation.

The CTBT has been explicitly identified by many nonnuclear-weapons states as their top priority in recent years. More specifically, it is what they demand out of the established nuclear powers as a condition for their continued willingness to forgo nuclear weapons themselves—while also agreeing to place their civilian nuclear programs under the additional protocol of the International Atomic Energy Association, or IAEA (which provides for thorough inspections of facilities). When the Nuclear Non-Proliferation Treaty was given an indefinite extension by the world community in 1995, it was achieved, according to the man who presided over the decisionmaking process, "largely because the long-stalled comprehensive test ban . . . seemed at last certain of adoption."[12] As such, the CTBT is directly linked to what many consider the top national security priority of the United States—stopping nuclear proliferation.

President Bush did not favor the CTBT. But with his presidency completed, treaty advocates can be relieved that he did nothing that irreversibly sank its prospects. President Bush did not "unsign" the treaty, as he was once purported to have considered doing; he also did not test nuclear weapons during his tenure in office. His administration periodically sought funds to research new types of nuclear warheads that would have likely required testing somewhere down the road, yet even the research efforts were severely constrained by Congress (as discussed more below, it is not clear that a different type of warhead would be a bad idea, if it could be developed and deployed without testing). Whatever harm that resulted to the nuclear nonproliferation regime during the last eight years, with the North Korean nuclear breakout in 2003 and its test in 2006 leading the way, was probably not primarily due to U.S. policy on nuclear testing. (It is worth recalling that even during the pro-CTBT Clinton administration, India and Pakistan became de facto nuclear powers, so the damage done to the global taboo on nuclear testing during this decade is roughly comparable to that of the previous decade.)

President Obama can and should push for CTBT ratification and implementation, a goal of nuclear arms control and nonproliferation advocates for half a century now. Yet, there are huge challenges to be addressed before any such agenda can be realized. At the U.S. domestic political level, although it was President Bush who wished to undo the CTBT, it was the Republican Senate of the late 1990s that opposed its ratification. The Republican caucus voted almost unanimously against the CTBT then; opposition was hardly limited to the most conservative members. Many avowed internationalists, who have often supported other treaties in the past and who value a U.S. foreign policy that promotes multilateralism and the pursuit of international consensus on key issues, voted against the CTBT. Former Republican secretaries of state George Schultz and Henry Kissinger are among those now favoring ratification, but many Republican senators are on record in opposition.[13] They raised questions that will have to be answered if a future CTBT ratification vote is to gain the support of ten to fifteen Republican members, the minimum that likely will be needed to ensure its passage and to establish a strong bipartisan support for a ban on nuclear testing in the future.

The key questions about the CTBT are these. Can such a treaty be verified? Does it really help enhance the nonproliferation agenda, and if so, how? Does it allow the United States to ensure the long-term reliability of its existing arsenal in a manner that provides robust deterrence for this country and its allies? Finally, to the extent that might be judged necessary, is the treaty consistent with future U.S. nuclear weapons needs? Each is considered below.

In pursuing CTBT ratification, advocates will have to be extremely careful in how they handle the question of pursuing complete nuclear disarmament discussed above. Abolition is not a bad idea in the abstract. Indeed, it is already in a sense U.S. policy, since it is explicitly advocated within the text of the NPT.[14] (That is, abolition is advocated assuming it can be done multilaterally and verifiably, with recourses for reconstitution of an international nuclear capability should extreme circumstances so warrant.[15]) But it is almost certainly not achievable in the coming decades. Implying otherwise can hurt the prospects of what is achievable—CTBT ratification—as well as related steps to lower nuclear danger such as further rounds of deep cuts in offensive arms and a fissile material cutoff treaty. Many if not most CTBT skeptics in the United States are worried that the treaty would weaken the U.S. nuclear deterrent, and given the state of international politics today, they see this as a major liability of the treaty, not a strength. Indeed, if the CTBT were to weaken the United States' nuclear deterrent in the short term, it *would* be a bad idea. Given the state of international politics, the world is not ready for nuclear abolition. (Indeed, Secretary of Defense Robert Gates was right in October 2008 to suggest a possible broadening rather than restricting of the United States' nuclear deterrence doctrine, pledging to hold "fully accountable" any country or group that helped terrorists obtain or employ weapons of mass destruction.[16]) As such, treaty skeptics must be reassured about the arsenal's robustness for the foreseeable future if there is to be any chance at ratification. CTBT advocates, therefore, must not conflate pursuit of treaty ratification with near-term pursuit of a nuclear abolition agenda. If they do so, they will stoke the very worries of treaty critics that must be addressed and countered if this critical accord is to be ratified by the U.S. Senate.

VERIFICATION

Large nuclear weapons detonations are easy to detect. If they are in the atmosphere (in violation of the atmospheric test ban treaty), they are visible from satellite, and their characteristic radiation distribution makes them easy to identify. It is for such reasons that no country trying to keep its nuclear capabilities secret has tested in the atmosphere in the modern era (South Africa is the last country that may have done so). If the detonations are underground, as is more common, it is still a straightforward process to identify them via seismic monitoring, provided they reach a certain size. Any weapon of kiloton power or above (the Hiroshima and Nagasaki bombs were in the 10 kiloton to 20 kiloton range) can be "heard" in this way. In other words, any weapon with significant military potential tested at its full strength is very likely to be noticed. U.S. seismic arrays are found throughout much of Eurasia's periphery, for example, and even tests elsewhere could generally be picked up. Indeed, even though it either "fizzled" or was designed to have a small yield in the first place, with a yield of under 1 kiloton and thus well below those of the Hiroshima and Nagasaki bombs, the North Korean test in October 2006 was detected and clearly identified as a nuclear burst.[17] Such sensitivity is expected worldwide as the International Monitoring System is further expanded (to include some 320 monitoring stations in ninety countries worldwide).[18] Indeed, it may be possible to detect tests less than one-tenth the power of the North Korean explosion.[19]

There are only two viable ways to escape detection. First, test a device well below its intended military yield, through some type of modification of the weapon's physics. (Doing this may in fact make the device very different from the actual class of weapon it is designed to represent, meaning that sophisticated extrapolation will be needed to deduce how the actual weapon would behave on the basis of the results of the detonation of the modified device.) Second, dig out a very large underground cavity into which a weapon can be placed, thereby "decoupling" the blast from direct contact with the ground and allowing it to weaken before it then reaches surrounding soil or rock and causes the earth to shake. This latter approach is arduous. And it does not make a weapon totally undetectable; it simply changes the threshold yield at which it can be heard by U.S., Russian, and international seismic sensors.[20] A country very sophisticated in nuclear technology might be able to do a test of a modified device that escaped international detection by virtue of having its normal yield reduced through modifications to the basic physics of the weapon. But accomplishing such engineering feats would probably be beyond the means of a fledgling power. They are in fact difficult even for advanced nuclear powers.

Nuclear verification capabilities have picked up the Indian, Pakistani, and North Korean nuclear tests—even the small, relatively unsuccessful ones—in the last decade and would be able to do so with high confidence for tests from those or other countries in the future. Verification capabilities are not airtight or perfect, but these limitations are hardly grounds to oppose a test ban treaty on balance.

THE CTBT AND NUCLEAR NONPROLIFERATION

It cannot really be true, critics of the CTBT sometimes argue, that an end to U.S. nuclear testing would stop proliferation—or testing by others. Surely Kim Jong Il of North Korea (DPRK), or President Ahmadinejad of Iran, or even the leaders of Pakistan and India are relatively unimpressed by any United States nuclear restraint. The first two tyrants are not easily inspired by acts of moral courage by other states. India and Pakistan, for their part, tend to argue that a country like the United States with thousands of nuclear warheads in its inventory and almost one thousand total nuclear tests under its belt is hardly in a position to deny others their nuclear rights. Any of these states, so goes the realist logic, will make nuclear-related decisions based much more on their own immediate security environments and agendas than out of concern about a global movement to limit the bomb's spread and to lower its profile.

These are serious objections. But while regional security conditions do matter more than global arguments for most countries contemplating the bomb, a strong international message against proliferation can still affect their calculations. If there is a sense that "everyone is doing it," leaders teetering on the edge of going nuclear will feel less restraint about doing so—and perhaps even an obligation to protect their own countries from the potential nuclear weapons of their neighbors. In this regard, maintaining a strong international dissuasive force against nuclearization is important, for it affects perceptions of the likelihood of proliferation. Indeed, efforts to delegitimize the bomb over the past half century and efforts to reduce testing and reduce arsenals over the last four decades have helped convince governments in places such as South Korea, Japan, Taiwan, Argentina, Chile, Brazil, Saudi Arabia, Egypt, and Germany not to pursue these weapons. Sometimes CTBT critics will trivialize these accomplishments, noting, for example, that it would not be so bad if a country like Japan or Brazil got the bomb anyway. But such arguments, even if partly right, ignore the fact that once one crosses the "nuclear tipping point" and momentum grows for getting the bomb around the world, it will not be just the Japans and Brazils from this list that go nuclear.[21]

Second, a CTBT would not physically prevent extremist states from getting the bomb, nor would it likely impress them with its moral force. But it would help reaffirm a norm, already acknowledged to a degree, that nuclear testing is unacceptable. This in turn will help discourage countries from testing the bomb out of fear that they will be punished if they do so. And if they test anyway, they will pay a price for it, which may convince them (or others) not to repeat the mistake and not to continue further down the same path.

Admittedly, this logic did not apply very well to the cases of India and Pakistan, which have hardly suffered serious and lasting reprisal from the world community as a result of their testing. As a generally stable and peaceful democracy, India's transgression was not viewed as anxiously as North Korea's by the international community. Pakistan's did raise major worries, but America's need to work with it in the struggle against extremists soon trumped the nonproliferation imperative. However, the world reaction to North Korea's October 2006 test, including a U.N. Security Council resolution limiting some types of world trade with North Korea, shows that this argument has some meaning. Norms do matter because they help in pressuring violators. Until its test, China and South Korea had largely protected the DPRK from severe sanctions, even after it broke out of the NPT in 2003. But when North Korea went so far as to test a bomb, Beijing and Seoul and Moscow told Pyongyang it had gone too far and agreed to economic reprisals against it.[22] It is also worth noting that Iran, for all of its efforts to develop nuclear technology, has shown some restraint to date and tried to dress up its activities under the guise of peaceful nuclear activities. Testing is inconsistent with such pretenses, meaning that Iran will likely think twice about testing even if it someday produces enough fissile material to be able to do so.

Or perhaps it will test just once, rather than five or ten times, making any resulting arsenal less reliable and quite possibly less sophisticated than it would otherwise be.

As far as we know, every country trying to validate a nuclear capability has succeeded on the first try. Simple fission bombs are relatively complicated devices, but generally not beyond the capacity of a country capable of enriching uranium or producing and reprocessing plutonium. However, developing advanced weapons—thermonuclear devices, devices capable of being delivered by missile, warheads capable of surviving atmospheric reentry and still performing correctly—is hard. Several countries including the United States have had difficulties, needing multiple tests and corrective procedures before establishing confidence with a given warhead design. Making it hard for proliferators to test will, therefore, among other benefits, make it harder for them to develop missile-mounted warheads of the type that would generally be most threatening against the United States and its allies.

THE CTBT AND STOCKPILE RELIABILITY

Most agree that the United States needs a nuclear deterrent well into the foreseeable future. Common sense would seem to support the position that, at some point at least, testing will be needed in the future to ensure the arsenal's reliability. How can one go 10 or 20 or 50 or 100 years without a single test and still be confident that the country's nuclear weapons will work? Equally important, how can one be sure that other countries will be deterred by a U.S. stockpile that at some point will be certified only by the experiments and tests of a generation of physicists long since retired or dead?

To be sure, with time, the reliability of a given warhead class may decline as its components age. In a worst case, it is conceivable that one category of warheads might in fact become flawed without our knowing it; indeed, this has happened in the past. But through a combination of monitoring, testing, and remanufacturing the individual components, conducting sophisticated experiments (short of actual nuclear detonations) on integrated devices, and perhaps introducing a warhead type or two of extremely conservative design into the inventory to complement existing types, the overall dependability of the U.S. nuclear deterrent can remain very good. In other words, there might be a slight reduction in the overall technical capacities of the arsenal, but still no question about its ability to exact a devastating response against anyone attacking the United States or its allies with weapons of mass destruction.

The Department of Energy has devoted huge sums of money to its stockpile stewardship program to understand as well as possible what happens within aging warheads and to predict the performance of those warheads once modified with slightly different materials in the future. It is a good program, and many experts now believe it will ensure the reliability of existing warheads for more than half a century. But there is still an element of theory to this approach that will give some unease; for example, a key part of the effort is using elegant three-dimensional computer models to predict what will happen inside a warhead modified to use a new type (or amount) of chemical explosive based on computational physics. This method is good but perhaps not perfect, especially over the longer term.[23]

A final way to ensure confidence in the arsenal is to design a different type of warhead or perhaps use an old design that is not currently represented in the active U.S. nuclear arsenal but that has been tested before. This approach would seek to use conservative designs that allow for slight errors in warhead performance and still produce a robust nuclear yield. Taking this approach might lead to a somewhat heavier warhead (meaning the number that could be carried on a given missile or bomber would have to be reduced), or a lower-yield warhead (meaning that a hardened Russian missile silo might not be so easily destroyed, for example). But for the purposes of post–cold war deterrence, this approach is generally sound, and weapons designers tend to agree that very reliable warheads can be produced if performance criteria are relaxed. It would also lead to less use of extremely toxic materials such as beryllium and safer types of conventional explosives (that are less prone to accidental detonation) than is the case for some warheads in the current arsenal.[24]

It is for such reasons that the Bush administration and Congress showed interest in a "reliable replacement warhead" (RRW) concept in the past few years. Secretary of Defense Robert Gates viewed it in effect as a precondition for U.S. ratification of the CTBT.[25] To date it is only a research concept, and a controversial one at that, with Congress not always willing to provide even research funding.[26] But while the RRW has become controversial, not only at home but abroad, the idea of building a conservative warhead design—based principally on old concepts, not new ones—probably makes sense on balance. Simple warhead designs are quite robust—recall that the Hiroshima bomb (a gun-assembly uranium device) was not even tested before being used, for example. As such, conservative designs could over time be added to the arsenal in modest numbers without testing—as a complement to current types, not as a complete substitute for them. There is no hurry about such a policy, except to keep workforces at the major labs focused and motivated. But it is an option worth retaining and probably pursuing in the coming years.

NEW NUCLEAR WEAPONS CAPABILITIES

Some have suggested that a reason to preserve our options for future nuclear testing relates to the potential need for new types of warheads to accomplish new missions. The idea of developing a nuclear weapon that could burrow underground *before* detonating has gained some recent appeal—not least because countries such as North Korea and Iran are responding to the United States' increasingly precise conventional weaponry by hiding key weapons programs well below the planet's surface.

One possible argument for such a warhead is to increase its overall destructive depth. In theory, the United States could modify the largest nuclear weapons in its stockpile to penetrate the earth. This approach would roughly double the destructive reach of the most powerful weapons in the current arsenal, according to physicist Michael Levi. But if an enemy can avoid weapons in the current arsenal, it could avoid the more powerful bombs by digging deeper underground. Given the quality of modern drilling equipment, that is not an onerous task.

Could earth-penetrating weapons at least reduce the nuclear fallout from an explosion? They could not prevent fallout; given limits on the hardness of materials and other basic physics, no useful nuclear weapon could penetrate the earth far enough to keep the radioactive effects of its blast entirely below ground. But such weapons could reduce fallout. As a rule of thumb, it is possible to reduce the yield of a weapon tenfold (or more) while converting it into an earth penetrator while maintaining the same destructive capability against underground targets that a normal weapon would have.[27] This would reduce fallout by a factor of ten as well.

That would be a meaningful change. But is it really enough to affect the basic usability of a nuclear device? Such a weapon would still produce a huge amount of fallout. Its use would still break the nuclear taboo. It would still only be capable of destroying underground targets if their locations were precisely known, in which case there is a chance that conventional weapons or special forces could neutralize the site.

Nuclear Testing and Nuclear Warhead Stewardship: Conclusion

A comprehensive test ban treaty makes very good strategic sense for the United States and the world. President Obama should build on Bill Clinton's signing of that treaty, as well as George W. Bush's tactic compliance with its strictures, and send it to the Senate for ratification. If it is not possible to gain congressional support for the treaty, the United States should nonetheless sustain its testing moratorium, even in the face of a test or two by another power (as undesirable as that would be).

What are the cost implications of this idea, coupled with a move toward a smaller nuclear arsenal? With a 1,000-warhead force not requiring testing, the United States need not have three major weapons laboratories devoted largely to oversight of the nuclear arsenal. Two would be adequate. In addition, it need not construct a dedicated new plutonium pit production facility; the modest capability at Los Alamos will suffice. Any building and deployment of a more conservative warhead design can happen gradually, in keeping with the limited capacities of the existing pit facility. These changes together allow average annual savings of about $1 billion in the Department of Energy's overall nuclear budget, which totals about $5 billion a year for weapons activities that include operating as well as construction costs.[28] About half of these savings would come from forgoing the new pit production facility and the other half from gradually ending the nuclear weapons research at one of the three main laboratories.[29]

Missile Defenses

Missile defense has been among the most polarizing and contentious issues in U.S. defense policy for a quarter century. It remains so today.

The Bush administration withdrew from the ABM Treaty in 2002 and proceeded to deploy ballistic missile defense systems—most notably, one for intercepting long-range warheads in the midcourse of their flight, which had been developed largely by the Clinton administration. As such, while the Bush administration was eager to withdraw from a treaty that the Clinton administration had had very mixed views about, the decision to deploy these systems had a certain bipartisan quality at some level (even as most Democrats objected to the way in which the Bush administration withdrew unilaterally and rather abruptly from the treaty).

Missile defense issues remain very important. The overall program is very expensive, averaging about $12 billion a year all told (including defenses against shorter-range missiles) during the Bush years. The request for 2009 was for $13 billion, and the longer-term plan forecast spending of $62.5 billion over the following five years.[30] Missile defense remains militarily very significant in a world of improving ballistic and cruise missile capabilities in the hands of several possible enemies of the United States. And missile defense remains very contentious in the U.S.-Russia relationship, most specifically at present over the proposed sites in Poland and the Czech Republic. The issue also causes concerns in Beijing, a major power with a much smaller nuclear arsenal than Russia's, which could in theory be countered to some extent by U.S. missile defenses, and also a power that could conceivably wind up in a serious crisis with the United States over the matter of Taiwan (even if that seems less likely at the moment). One need not oppose missile defense categorically, wish for a restoration of the ABM Treaty, or sympathize with any and all criticisms of missile defense by foreign governments to recognize the sensitivities of the issue.

Several programs are at the core of the current U.S. missile defense effort. They include the Patriot missile (for a ground-based defense against missiles in the final or "terminal" stage of flight), THAAD (Terminal High Altitude Area Defense, a ground-based defense against midcourse threats of modest range), the Alaska-California system (a ground-based defense, with help from sea-based radar, against long-range missile threats), the Navy Aegis system (against missile threats over or near the sea), and the airborne laser as well as the kinetic energy interceptor (both designed to work against missiles in their boost phase, just after launch and while they are still burning). In addition, many of these specific systems are being linked together and fed information by various command and control systems, radar programs (upgrades to existing radars and deployment of new ones), and the planned launch of a major satellite constellation to track warheads (and try to identify them if disguised within clouds of decoys or other countermeasures). These various types of capabilities also are being upgraded more or less continuously.

At this point, the Missile Defense Agency has now upgraded radars on land in Japan, the United Kingdom, Alaska, and California and built a sea-based mobile radar homeported in Alaska. In the course of 2009, it will have eighteen Aegis-class ships with the capability to intercept medium-range missiles and a total of thirty-four Standard Missile–3 (SM-3) interceptors on them. The agency has conducted thirty-five successful hit-to-kill intercepts in forty-three attempts, with various degrees of realism in those tests.[31] The money devoted to missile defense in 2009 is intended to purchase more midcourse interceptors for the Alaska-California system, to go to a total of forty-four; another 100 SM interceptors for the Navy Aegis system; additional THAAD interceptors making for a total of 100 to date; additional Patriot missiles making for some 500 to date; and initial construction on the system based in Europe if desired.[32] It will also permit continued upgrades of radars.[33] Other improvements are expected as well—for example, new missiles (one being developed with Japan) within the Navy SM-3 program that have a greater range and speed as well as more capable two-color, infrared sensors for tracking.[34]

Missile defense systems were often pilloried for pursuing unrealistic technology and "rushing to failure" in previous years. Technologies were too grandiose, such as proposals for giant lasers in space with their beams steered to target via telescope-like mirrors, and too hurried, with programs structured on a crash basis. In recent years programs have been somewhat more realistic, and also more successful, at least against simple threats.

Yet important questions remain about whether any missile defense system can really work against a sophisticated enemy. It would face two huge, inherent challenges under such circumstances: First, an attacker would not need to get all or even most nuclear-tipped missiles through a defense to be successful, and second, relatively simple countermeasures can mimic actual warheads or otherwise spoof sensors, making it very hard for a defense to know which incoming objects are true threats and which are not. While a defender can always develop methods of discrimination, attackers can always further improve the quality of their decoys, and on balance the interactions would seem to favor the attacker, especially in the vacuum of space where the weight of any warhead could not be easily used to distinguish it from a decoy. (That said, it is not obvious that a country like North Korea could afford enough missile flight tests to perfect decoys; nor would it have an easy time carrying them out in terms of the likely international political reaction. In fact, in an otherwise successful test in 2008, the United States itself attempted to deploy countermeasures on a ballistic missile, but the countermeasures failed to function properly.[35]) Leaving aside the possibility of sophisticated decoys, missile defense systems to date have often not even been proven to work at night, or against a reentry vehicle that tumbles rather than falling straight (tumbling makes the flight less predictable), or against decoys even generally resembling real warheads.[36]

In light of a missile defense's uncertain technical attributes, and the huge expense involved in purchasing multiple and redundant systems, some programs could be slowed. The list might include the airborne laser, which has demonstrated recent progress in several ground tests but is of uncertain near-term technological ripeness (with actual flight tests against simulated targets scheduled for late 2009); the space-based missile tracking satellite constellation, for a similar reason; the next round of planned expansions of the midcourse missile defense; and any advanced development of the kinetic energy interceptor missile.[37] Postponements would not necessarily be "punishment" for poor performance; the Airborne Laser program, for example, appears to be progressing reasonably well.[38] Rather, at some point, the question becomes one of affordability and efficiency. A certain amount of redundancy is appropriate in missile defense, given the high stakes, but building THAAD and Navy Aegis and airborne laser systems all at once may verge on the excessive, simply on the grounds of budgetary costs and opportunity costs.

Even with such decisions, missile defense efforts would remain expensive, in the range of $10 billion a year instead of $12 billion to $13 billion—and still well above the inflation-adjusted levels of the Reagan years that were in the range of $6 billion (in 2009 dollars).[39] To put this in more specific terms as used by the Pentagon's Missile Defense Agency, while its first two phases (known as Block 1.0 and 2.0) would be completed more or less as now intended, Blocks 3.0, 4.0, and 5.0 would be substantially slowed—and as each is estimated to cost about $1 billion a year, the cumulative annual savings might reach $2 billion. The overall effort would still be expensive, but it would be forced to observe fiscal discipline. Secretary Gates's plan appears similar to mine.

Consider in more detail one specific planned missile defense system. The Bush administration during its last years in office worked to promote a new ballistic missile defense capability in Poland and the Czech Republic. The system—which would complement the one established in recent years in California and Alaska—is intended primarily to protect Europe and the United States from a missile launched from the Middle East. It is, in principle, a worthy idea, but the military benefits in the short term are not worth the worsening of relations with Russia that it has already engendered. President Obama should take a year or two to develop patiently a plan for deployment, rather than rush to follow through on the current schedule.

As now planned, the system would consist of a single radar on Czech soil and just ten interceptor missiles in Poland. Many NATO states support the general idea of a missile defense system. Yet, they have wondered why Washington originally decided to pursue this plan primarily as a two-track process with only Poland and the Czech Republic—two new, modest-sized members of the alliance—given its broader significance for NATO as a whole.

A bigger question may be why the United States was in such a hurry to get this system going under President Bush, especially given its inherent limitations. The ten interceptor missiles could in theory intercept only ten warheads and in all probability would do well to destroy a couple. Given the short amount of time available to destroy a missile launched from the Middle East—likely no more than twenty minutes—we would probably have to fire several of the missiles at once to destroy a single warhead, as there would be no time to wait and see if an initial interceptor hit its mark. In addition, we all know the problems the military has had in testing missiles for the Pacific missile shield, and the interceptors to be used in Central Europe are going to operate, in part, on a different, even less-proven technology.

The flip side of the weaknesses of the antimissile system is that Russia's objections to it are without serious strategic merit.[40] Russia has hundreds of ballistic missiles; thus in the unthinkable event of a nuclear war between it and the West, the Central European defense system would be like using a fly swatter against a bazooka. (Not to mention that Russia could do what a rogue regime might not have the technology to accomplish: deploying countermeasures that could make the small system entirely useless. For example, the antimissile program might well be fooled by missiles that release several decoys after they leave the atmosphere.)

But the fact of the matter is that Russia does object to the plan, many European allies are nervous, and the whole idea is associated with Bush administration unilateralism. Any major decision to build a new defense system needs to recognize this perception and factor it into the strategic and diplomatic calculus.

We should also involve Russia even more in the discussion. Moscow should not have a veto. But its perspective does matter, especially as good diplomacy might be able to turn it into a supporter rather than an opponent of the plan. Perhaps insincerely, Putin has shown some flexibility on the subject, proposing joint development of a defense system that could make use of a Soviet-built radar in Azerbaijan and another on Russian territory. These ideas may be clever means of appearing reasonable without any real commitment to the notion of joint missile defense—but they are not unserious technically and are worth pursuing, at least as an element of a European defense system.[41]

President Obama will carry far less baggage than his predecessor, Mr. Bush, who worsened his image in regard to this issue by formalizing an arrangement with Poland to host the missiles in the heat of the August 2008 Georgia crisis—with his press secretary then declaring that the timing was "mostly coincidental." That comment was ill-advised, since it seemed to validate Moscow's belief that the system is in fact directed against Russia (even though this is not true). Given the gradual pace at which any threat is materializing and the relative slowness with which our technology is advancing, this is clearly a matter where haste makes waste. Most important, we must bear in mind that, as Secretary of Defense Robert Gates reminded Mr. Putin last year, "One cold war was quite enough."

On balance, the changes suggested above would reduce the annual missile defense budget substantially—as noted, by perhaps $2 billion a year—though it would remain very large compared with the Reagan, the first Bush, and the Clinton levels.

CHAPTER FOUR

CONVENTIONAL MILITARY FORCES AND OPERATIONS

As DISCUSSED IN CHAPTER 2, the lion's share of U.S. military spending is accounted for by the main combat formations, weapons, and activities of the four military services. They are sized to be capable of two intense regional wars or protracted stabilization missions of the type ongoing in Iraq and Afghanistan, to maintain presence and thereby to foster deterrence of great-power conflict in places including the Western Pacific and Persian Gulf and Central Europe, and to retain a qualitative edge that discourages challengers from attempting to reach parity with the United States while also reassuring allies. After two decades of post–cold war honing, the force postures of the services are fairly well streamlined for these purposes (though some additional modest changes are suggested below). (See table 4-1 for a list countries where U.S. troops are currently based.) However, weapons acquisition accounts, focused as they are on hypothetical future threats and needs, have probably not been as carefully scrutinized in some cases. Some are too ambitious and too costly. That is one theme that guides the pages in this chapter.

Several of the following topics revolve around one military service or another. But two broader subjects begin and end the chapter. The first, peacekeeping, stabilization, and humanitarian intervention, relates primarily to decisions on Army and Marine Corps force structure, but it merits focused attention in its own right. The other, overseas military basing, concerns all the services.

PEACEKEEPING AND HUMANITARIAN INTERVENTION

More than half a million people a year have been dying in the world's conflicts in places such as Darfur and the Congo this decade.[1] This ongoing tragedy underscores the need for greater global military, as well as police and civilian, capacities to stabilize troubled lands. This is important not only on humanitarian grounds, but also in light of the fact that conflict-prone states often provide havens to terrorists and sources of other global problems such as the illicit narcotics trade and the spread of infectious diseases. It is time to focus on what David Gompert of RAND has called "capacity to protect," given that international law and politics have increasingly recognized a "responsibility to protect" (or R2P, in the vernacular of the business).[2] If it is incumbent on the world community to do what is possible to stop deadly conflict, we must have the means to do so. It is time to go beyond R2P and develop C2P.

One ongoing crisis is in the Congo. That conflict, responsible perhaps for up to several million deaths in the last decade and also responsible for probably the world's worst sexual violence today, continues to cause acute problems in eastern Congo. A Tutsi warlord, Nkunda, and his CNDP movement have wreaked havoc despite the presence of U.N. peacekeepers and Congolese army forces. Nkunda has now been arrested, with the fate of his organization uncertain. But government forces remain noteworthy for corruption and violence themselves, as are multiple militias. Worst of all is the group composed largely of former Hutu *genocidaires* from the Rwanda tragedy of 1994, making up the FDLR. Neighboring Rwanda's sustained and enduring commitment to hold Nkunda is unclear. Rwanda is motivated at least in part by the view that the Hutu extremists linked to the 1994 genocide will thrive in that part of the Congo if not checked by Rwanda's army and its surrogates. With the east in turmoil, the rest of the Congo cannot easily progress very fast, and the broader region remains jeopardized by conflict in this huge state bordering nine different African nations.

What to do? Diplomacy certainly has a key place. What the region also needs, however, is a sufficiently strong international security presence to protect civilian populations—and, over time, to help train the Congolese

TABLE 4-1. U.S. Troops Based in Foreign Countries[a]
(as of December 31, 2008)

Country or region	Number of troops	Country or region	Number of troops
Europe		*Sub-Saharan Africa*	
Belgium	1,256	Djibouti	1,349
Germany	41,674	Other	294
Italy	8,660	*Subtotal*	1,643
Netherlands	541		
Portugal	778	*Western Hemisphere*	
Serbia (includes Kosovo)	1,120	Cuba (Guantanamo)	953
Spain	1,230	Other	1,086
Turkey	1,559	*Subtotal*	2,039
United Kingdom	8,857		
Afloat	692	Subtotal: all foreign	138,348
Other	915	countries, not including	
Subtotal	67,282	war deployments	
Former Soviet Union	133	War deployments: all	209,700
		Operation Iraqi Freedom	178,300
East Asia & Pacific		Operation Enduring	31,400
Japan	31,189	Freedom	
Korea	24,555		
Afloat	7,387		
Other	669	Total currently abroad	348,048
Subtotal	63,800		
North Africa, Near East and South Asia			
Bahrain	1,467		
Afloat	420		
Other	1,564		
Subtotal	3,451		

Source: Department of Defense, "Active Duty Military Personnel Strengths by Regional Area and by Country" website (http://siadapp.dmdc.osd.mil/personnel/MILITARY/history/hst0812.pdf).

a. Only countries with at least 500 troops are listed individually. About 17,250 troops were deployed to the wars from usual bases abroad: 13,300 from Germany, 2,850 from Japan, 500 from the United Kingdom, 500 from Italy, and 100 from South Korea.

military so that it can do a better job on its own. The international community needs a larger, stronger force than the 17,500 total personnel making up MONUC (*Mission de l'Organisation des Nations Unies du Congo*) at present.[3] The additional 3,000 or so soldiers authorized by the United Nations for the mission in November of 2008 may or may not be enough—right now the key goal is to get them to the field, properly trained and equipped, expeditiously.

A second key case is Darfur. For years, patience has been the world's watchword as the Darfur tragedy unfolds. Whoever is most to blame for the conflict of late—Sudan's government, or the government as well as the rebels—it is the innocent people of the region who suffer, with a quarter million or more believed to have perished in the last half decade. The international presence in Darfur has remained under 10,000 troops even as the need has been recognized as at least twice that—not to mention the need for more robust rules of engagement for those troops.

With U.S. troops so badly overcommitted in Iraq and Afghanistan, and with worries that any U.S. presence would give Osama bin Laden more talking points about "infidels" purportedly invading Islamic lands and fighting Muslim governments, even American progressives have tended to shy away from recommending deployment of U.S. forces on the ground. (Similar arguments apply to Somalia, where the United States has had a bad recent experience, and from where the United States could face a threat from terrorists that use the anarchic country for sanctuary.) This means that the United States' main short-term role in any reinforcement of this mission may, as with the Congo, be in the domain of improved support for international troops, particularly those from Africa, to help them perform the mission more effectively.

Over the medium term, the Obama administration may have other policy options, as discussed below. For crises like the Congo and Darfur, the United States should consider a radical innovation in recruiting policy. We should create a genocide prevention and peace operations division in the U.S. Army with individuals enlisting specifically for this purpose. There would be risks in such a venture, to be sure. But they are manageable and tolerable risks, especially since most such deployments would be legitimated by the United Nations, carried out with partners such as key allies, and backstopped by the U.S. armed forces in worst-case scenarios.

The notion is this: of all those well-intentioned and admirable Americans rallying to call attention to Darfur and demand action, ask for volunteers to join a genocide prevention and peace operations division for two years. They would begin their service with roughly twelve weeks of boot camp and twelve weeks of specialized training and then would be deployable. They would receive the same compensation and health benefits as regular troops, given their age and experience; other incentives such as educational assistance would be made roughly proportionate to their length of service.

This training regimen would be modeled after standard practices in today's Army and Marine Corps. To be sure, soldiers and marines in regular units usually go beyond this regimen to have many months of additional practice and exercising before being deployed. Moreover, within their units, at any given moment most personnel are well into their first tour or on their second or third enlistments (the average soldier or marine in today's armed forces has more than five years of military experience).

By contrast, many genocide prevention and peace operations soldiers could be much greener when sent into action. Some of them would have to be older and more experienced, however. For example, former military officers could volunteer—taking positions of leadership within the new force structure.

There would be risks with this kind of division, to be sure. But there are several reasons why the associated risks would be acceptable—even if a peace accord in a country where they deploy breaks down or does not exist in the first place. First, those volunteering for the new division would understand the associated risks and accept them. Second, in most civil conflicts, possible adversarial forces are not sophisticated. Soldiers in the new division would not need to execute complex operations akin to those carried out during the invasion of Iraq or current operations in Iraq and Afghanistan. They would largely monitor villages and refugee camps, inspect individuals to make sure they did not have illicit weapons, and call for help if they ever came under concerted attack. Their jobs could be somewhat dangerous and would require discipline and reasonable knowledge of some basic infantry skills—but they would not be extremely complex. Care would have to be taken in deciding when to deploy this force—but it generally would be, given the scars of recent, difficult American experiences in places such as Somalia.

Third, the new force would have some direct backup from standard U.S. military units if needed. In other words, the mission could admittedly impose some slight additional strain on an Army and Marine Corps already heavily overdeployed abroad. But such U.S. main combat forces would probably not have to be larger than company-size formations—200 to 300 troops each. Assuming several such companies would be deployed, perhaps 1,000 U.S. soldiers and Marines from existing units would be needed countrywide in a possible near-term deployment to the Congo or Darfur or elsewhere, to back up several thousand new enlistees in the dedicated force. In addition, U.S. airpower in the form of Air Force jets or other assets could help back up the units, as might Navy helicopters (which are not being quite as severely stressed in the Iraq operation as are many other types of formations).

Problems like the Congo, Darfur, and Somalia only tend to get solved with U.S. leadership. And the United States cannot truly lead on this issue while resisting any role for its own ground forces. It is time to recognize the contradiction of pretending otherwise and get on with a solution.

The nature of this division would allow for a smaller size, since it would not employ the full range of combat capabilities normally associated with a U.S. Army division. Assuming some 10,000 soldiers for the division itself, and a comparably sized support base, the average annual costs of these 20,000 additional soldiers would be about $3 billion a year.

Of course, this new genocide prevention and peace operations force would not be the preferred military instrument in many cases. Ongoing U.S. efforts to help other countries expand their peace enforcement and peacekeeping capacities should continue and intensify. Other countries' forces are typically much less expensive, and the international community on the whole typically shares in their deployment costs. In addition, when they are deployed, U.S. troops are not put in danger—or, at a minimum, others share in the danger. It is worth sketching out the broader agenda here, as part of a multilateral effort that places the above U.S. initiatives in context.

Since the late 1990s, the United States has carried out programs to help African states in particular with their capacity to handle such missions more effectively. Beginning with a dedicated program to help Nigerian forces assist in stabilizing Liberia, then generalizing to what was called the Africa Crisis Response Initiative in the Clinton administration (and the Africa Contingency Operations Training and Assistance program in the Bush administration), the idea has been to train modest numbers of African army formations in the basics of such efforts. The programs began very modestly, with annual funding in the range of $10 million and severe restrictions on the type of (nonlethal) equipment that could be transferred. Concerns that such programs could be seen as equipping countries to abuse their own indigenous populations or their neighbors limited the initial enthusiasm, as did worries that they would be seen as just another foreign aid program. But over the years, the logic of helping Africans in particular better defend their continent's own peoples rightly has been seen to trump these other considerations, and as such the combined efforts have grown to approach $100 million a year in funding. This U.S. program is similar to efforts by Canada, France, Britain, and Italy in comparable programs. It uses one or two Special Forces soldiers (or contractors) per every 100 foreign forces—often focusing its main efforts on training the trainers rather than indigenous troops themselves.[4]

Still, the scale of the need remains very large. As of 2007, about 150,000 troops were deployed in global peace operations.[5] That total figure included roughly 73,000 under U.N. auspices, plus almost another 10,000 police deployed under U.N. auspices. In addition to the U.N. missions, there were also 56,000 troops under NATO command; the rest were led by the African Union, European Union, and other generally regional organizations. This level of global effort reflected substantial growth even relative to the late 1990s when NATO was so heavily engaged in the Balkans (and total troops deployed were around 120,000). While there have been ups and downs throughout the post–cold war period, the overall trends show no signs of abating. In fact, current missions in Darfur, the Congo, and Afghanistan remain undermanned according to the views of most experts.[6] Even relative to authorized levels, U.N. missions were about 18,000 troops short in 2008; there were also severe gaps in police and in civilian support personnel.[7]

It is no accident that many of the most underresourced peace operations are in Africa. Moreover, ongoing instability in the Horn of Africa in particular raises the prospect of even more need for such missions in the years ahead.

Putting all of this together, in light of current needs and recent trends, the international community should prepare for the possibility, if not the likelihood, of deploying and sustaining up to 200,000 troops overseas at a time. In fact, the number could easily grow larger yet in the event of a truly catastrophic development such as a collapsing Pakistan, Indonesia, or Nigeria that felt the need to ask for help as it lost control over some or much of its territory. However unlikely such scenarios, they cannot be discounted entirely, and the strategic significance of some (especially of a dissolving nuclear-armed Pakistan) would be such that the world could hardly stand idly by as events unfolded.[8]

Fielding 200,000 troops at a time would require perhaps 600,000 available troops in a global rotation base. (Missions could last several years, and no individual soldier should be asked to stay in the field for much more than a year in general.) Assuming that most of these forces should not be American, largely because these types of missions are of importance to all, not just the United States and its key allies, this can be translated into a set of regional goals for various countries, continents, and regional organizations.

This math suggests that existing training and equipping programs should expand considerably, a goal with which a recent Genocide Prevention Task Force led by Madeleine Albright and William Cohen appears to agree.[9] If there is any doubt about the need for more effort, and more resources, the fact that the United States has spent some $20 billion to date training and equipping the 500,000-strong Iraqi Security Forces should help reinforce the point (Iraqis have spent many billions of their own money as well).[10] With a funding level for the Global Peace Operations Initiative of about $100 million a year, some 40,000 troops have been trained to date, with an overall worldwide goal of 75,000 (see table 4-2). The program is too small by a factor of two to three, and its intensity—measured in just days of training, as well as modest amounts of equipment transferred—is comparably underfinanced. The program should be roughly tripled in size, and actual combat equipment as well as nonlethal aid should be selectively included as well. The $100 million a year figure should grow to $500 million (these costs result from the above military analysis, but they would be foreign assistance costs and as such are recorded in the summary table under the 150 budget).[11] Western nations should do more too, though their efforts would not involve U.S. budgetary resources and as such are not discussed in detail here.[12]

U.S. ARMY FORCE STRUCTURE AND PERSONNEL

The U.S. Army is growing by about 70,000 active duty soldiers in an overdue policy change long resisted by Secretary Rumsfeld but now promoted by Congress and Secretary Gates. In so doing, it is building forty-five brigade combat teams in the active force, and a total of some

TABLE 4-2. Military Peacekeepers Trained by Global Peacekeeping Operations Initiative[a]
(as of April 2008)

GPOI partner	Peacekeepers trained	Peacekeepers deployed
Africa		
Benin	2,519	2,053
Botswana	165	0
Burkina Faso	1,890	0
Cameroon	12	0
ECOWAS[b]	288	0
Gabon	1,393	202
Ghana	3,853	2,920
Kenya	86	39
Malawi	1,073	0
Mali	997	0
Mozambique	1,029	0
Namibia	882	0
Niger	1,157	666
Nigeria	4,988	3,758
Rwanda	4,903	4,811
Senegal	7,888	6,833
South Africa	243	98
Tanzania	971	55
Uganda	1,955	0
Zambia	676	0
Subtotal Africa	36,968	21,435
Asia		
Bangladesh	128	0
Brunei[c]	6	0
Cambodia	173	0
Fiji	47	0
India[c]	47	45
Indonesia	208	0
Laos[c]	1	0
Malaysia	116	0
Mongolia	629	497
Nepal	11	0
Philippines	8	0
Singapore[c]	10	0
Sri Lanka	58	0
Thailand	278	0
Tonga[c]	85	19
Subtotal Asia	1,805	561

GPOI partner	Peacekeepers trained	Peacekeepers deployed
South and Central America		
Belize	2	0
El Salvador	24	0
Guatemala	306	0
Honduras	87	0
Nicaragua	36	0
Subtotal Central and South America	455	0
Europe		
Albania	254	0
Bosnia and Herzegovina	1	0
Ukraine	34	0
Subtotal Europe	289	0
Near East and Central Asia		
Jordan	1	0
Subtotal Near East and Central Asia	1	0
Total	39,518	21,996[d]

Source: GAO, *Peacekeeping: Thousands Trained but United States Is Unlikely to Complete All Activities by 2010 and Some Improvements Are Needed*, GAO-08-754 (June 2008), pp. 46–48 (www.gao.gov/new.items/d08754.pdf).

ECOWAS = Economic Community of West African States; GPOI = Global Peacekeeping Operations Initiative.

a. According to the U.S. State Department, these peacekeepers have been deployed to twelve United Nations or African Union (AU) missions, as well as other unspecified missions not supported by the UN or AU.

b. Training for ECOWAS was for the commander and staff of the Standby Force Headquarters. Multiple countries participated in these exercises.

c. Brunei, India, Laos, Singapore, and Tonga did not receive GPOI funds, but they sent peacekeepers to be trained during GPOI-funded events.

d. GPOI has also provided deployment equipment and transportation to support the deployment of 4,680 military peacekeepers from Indonesia, Kenya, Nigeria, and Uganda, and an unspecified number of military peacekeepers from Chile and Guatemala. In addition, 229 military peacekeepers from Mongolia deployed to Afghanistan and Iraq, and 343 military peacekeepers deployed to Afghanistan from the South-Eastern Europe Brigade of the Multinational Peace Force South-East Europe.

seventy-five including National Guard units. It is also creating a total of about 225 support brigades among active, National Guard, and reserve units.[13]

This policy makes sense because it is possible that current wars will not wind down quickly. In addition, for tired soldiers and marines on their second or third or fourth tours, the nation should send a message that it is trying to spread their burden among more troops, even if it is doing so belatedly. More than 50,000 troops have already done three deployments to Iraq, and that number is growing fast.[14] Other scenarios, such as stabilization or peacekeeping missions in Africa and South Asia, could also impose demands on U.S. forces as well as on those of other countries. And whatever progress is made in increasing stabilization, development, and nation building capacities in other parts of government, the progress will be gradual in pace and modest in scale. So the Department of Defense will have to bear a large fraction of the future burden too.[15]

In building a larger Army and Marine Corps, missions like those in Iraq and Afghanistan should remain the focal point of DoD's efforts. The future U.S. Army must never again relegate missions like counterinsurgency and complex peace operations to the categories of being unimportant, unrewarding, unlikely, or "lesser included" types of military operations (with traditional combat being the only main driver of force sizing and training). The Iraq and Afghanistan conflicts should have taught us that. This has important implications not only for special forces but for main combat formations in the U.S. Army and Marine Corps as well.

In fact, the Department of Defense recognized as much four years into the Afghanistan operation and two and a half years into the Iraq war, while Donald Rumsfeld was still secretary of defense. His November 2005 directive, DoD Directive 3000.05, stated the following:

> Stability operations are a core U.S. military mission that the Department of Defense shall be prepared to conduct and support. They shall be given priority comparable to combat operations and be explicitly addressed and integrated across all DoD activities including doctrine, organizations, training, education, exercises, materiel, leadership, personnel, facilities, and planning.

A major Army manual released in October 2008 repeated the same message, underscoring that stability operations were as important to U.S. ground forces as both classic offense and classic defense and were perhaps more likely to determine the outcome of a complex military mission than either of these other types of operations.[16] The National Intelligence Council concurs that irregular warfare will only increase in frequency, making such U.S. operations continuously relevant.[17]

This premise has two types of implications for the U.S. military. One concerns the training of the main combat forces, the other concerns the specialized roles of units devoted principally to counterinsurgency, stabilization missions, and peace operations.

TRAINING MAIN COMBAT FORMATIONS IN THE ARMY AND MARINE CORPS

As long as the Iraq and Afghanistan operations remain so important and intense, units preparing to deploy will naturally focus first and foremost on preparations for the challenges they will face in these missions. Some in the Army and Marine Corps object, voicing concerns about the deterioration of traditional combat skills, as discussed above in the section on readiness.[18] But while theoretically valid, this point cannot carry the day when soldiers and marines are putting their lives on the line in counterinsurgency and stabilization missions abroad. The United States military retains enough institutional excellence in heavy air-land battle from periods through 2003, and it also remains battle-hardened enough from ongoing operations since then, that its overall combat readiness likely remains rather solid.

But what about the medium-term future? As the wars gradually wind down (or at least, as their cumulative burden on the ground forces declines), how should the Army and Marine Corps train their forces? How do we stay prepared for counterinsurgency, stabilization, and "low-intensity" operations when also trying to restore some level of proficiency with major armored maneuver and other traditional operations? The Army is now functioning on a different readiness model than it did before, more like the Navy–Marine Corps pattern of having a certain fraction of units (but not all) ready at a given time. This new model makes sense for the long term too. With this readiness model, how should the military balance different missions and different types of preparations?

One way to think about the future challenge is to imagine four categories of training for units in the future: ongoing work on basic skills, training in small-unit tactics for traditional combat, training in small-unit tactics for counterinsurgency and peace operations, and training in larger units for traditional combat. It is difficult to say that a given year's training should allocate equal time to each of these; my point is more general. Training should allocate roughly equal *priority* to each of these four. Clearly, the military services will have to be the ones to develop specific plans of action, but their broad philosophy should accord importance to all these areas.

NEW, SPECIALIZED UNITS

In addition to balancing training, the future Army and Marine Corps need to readjust their force structures somewhat. Four new types of units should be seriously considered in future Army force structure in particular. One has already been discussed: a dedicated peacekeeping–genocide prevention division.

The other three initiatives should include the creation of an Army advisory corps for training foreign militaries including in the use of equipment acquired through military assistance channels, an increase in certain kinds of high-demand–low-density units outside of main combat structures that are heavily employed in today's armed forces, and a dedicated homeland security brigade in the Army National Guard.

Retired Lt. Col. John Nagl has become a major champion of the Army Advisory Corps. He envisions a 20,000-strong corps, organized into three divisions, with further subdivisions designed to give officers serving in this corps strong credentials when future promotion decisions are made and to give the advisory function prominence within theater command structures. (The corps would be led by a lieutenant general, each division would be led by a major general typically deploying abroad with his units.) Nagl's attentiveness to such command matters is shared by Secretary Gates, who has argued, "One of the enduring issues our military struggles with is whether personnel and promotions systems designed to reward command of U.S. troops will be able to reflect the importance of advising, training, and equipping foreign troops—which is still not considered a career enhancing path for our best and brightest officers."[19] This situation must change, and our national capacity to train foreign militaries must increase.

The overall size of Nagl's proposed Advisory Corps is roughly commensurate with recent demands. To wit, in Iraq the United States has been using almost 6,000 military personnel to train Iraqi army and police teams—not quite enough for all major units in the half million–strong Iraqi Security Forces, but of the right magnitude. Not all Iraqi units will need help indefinitely, moreover, so this sizing is perhaps a good basis for future planning. Factoring in the Afghanistan mission, if properly sized it could also require more than 5,000 U.S. trainers (in teams of 15 to 25 per brigade, translating into 300 or more teams per country). Some of these demands could be handled by the special forces normally charged with such work. As such, Nagl's 20,000 figure would seem about right, providing a rotation base for missions lasting more than a couple of years.

However, smaller numbers of trainers could play a useful role too. In principle one need not train an entire foreign military at this level of intensity simultaneously—and one hopes that in the future there may not be two major simultaneous efforts either.[20] Moreover, there is a case that specialized trainers are most important in places where the United States is *not* carrying out large-scale military operations of its own, or as supplements to fill manpower gaps in places like Iraq and Afghanistan. In the latter circumstances, main combat forces can perhaps continue to handle much of the challenge, since they will have experience in country as well as the kinds of relationships with indigenous partners needed to make such collaboration successful. In fact, this is the thinking behind the security cooperation BCT (brigade combat team) concept—the Army's present paradigm—by which a main brigade force (or some fraction of it) can be assigned to training purposes temporarily in a place where it has already functioned in a more traditional manner.[21] On balance, a mix of Nagl's idea with existing concepts is probably most sound, and additional funding for perhaps 5,000 more trainers at an annual cost of about $500 million would be the right scale of effort.

A second issue as noted concerns so-called high-demand–low-density (HD-LD) units—which include military police, engineering units, and civil affairs specialists. These units are often overtaxed in complex operations such as those in Iraq and Afghanistan.[22] A careful assessment by Robert Martinage of the Center for Strategic and Budgetary Assessments advocates increases of roughly 4,000 uniformed personnel in these areas, largely in civil affairs and psychological operations specialties. He also supports procurement of more than 150 support aircraft, with a total price tag perhaps in the range of $2 billion (to be spread over a number of years), for the increased special operations forces.[23] These recommendations seem generally sound.

One other area in which further changes seem appropriate still is in dedicated homeland security capabilities. Some ideas here have gone too far. The United States needs its National Guard too much for war fighting, for example, to devote it strictly to homeland security missions—which are highly unlikely ever to require several hundred thousand uniformed personnel in any event (and in fact have generally used well under 10 percent of that amount in the past). However, a dedicated unit, perhaps of brigade size, serving as a first responder, a center of excellence, and a center of training, as well as a coordinator for the nation's broader military and police capabilities, does make sense. Such a unit could have a battalion of capability (about 1,000 troops) on call at all times and be able to put more people on alert under certain circumstances (such as the approach of a known severe hurricane). It could work with Northern Command to ensure that plans for moving military forces and other national assets into various types of disaster zones were well established. It could foster regional coordination across National Guard bureaucracies to smooth and speed the process by which one state could aid another in a crunch. It could also ensure that key technologies—interoperable radios, chemical protective suits, and so on—were properly developed, purchased, and deployed. And it would always be available for domestic purposes, at the beck and call of the president.[24]

PAY AND COMPENSATION

It is appropriate at a time when men and women in uniform are doing so much for the country to ask if more can and should be done to help them. The starting point should be a realization that military pay, while never truly enough to compensate those who actively risk their lives for their country, is nonetheless reasonably good by comparison with private sector jobs for individuals of comparable age, experience, and education.[25] But this is hardly the end of the story. And while recruiting and retention trends are better than before, they have shown enough fragility in recent years to warrant ongoing policy attention.

One additional reform could involve military pension plans. The military retirement system is essentially an "all or nothing" operation. Stay in for twenty years and become fully vested and immediately eligible for full benefits; stay in a day less and receive nothing. This approach probably hurts retention for those considering whether to stay in the military or not as they approach five to ten years of service. That is the period when another few years of military employment promise no accrued pension benefits whatsoever (unless personnel wind up staying the full twenty years), yet it is when private sector jobs generally would begin to vest them quickly. The military should probably keep its core retirement system but offer a modest 401k-like option to help those not planning on a twenty-year career. This idea may be considered simply as a matter of fairness, or of keeping up with the times and the changing nature of the U.S. economy.[26] Traditional pension plans could be debited by a corresponding amount for anyone who did stay twenty years. If a matching payment of up to $1,000 a year was instituted, for example, and one million troops took advantage, the cost would be $1 billion a year.

Several other specific benefits to troops should still be improved, even after the progress of recent years. For example, wage compensation should be offered to spouses or parents who have to quit their jobs to care for a severely disabled veteran. Veterans waiting for initial benefits packages and still unemployed shortly upon returning home should also have financial bridging options, especially if injured.[27] The number of people requiring such help in any given year might total 10,000 to 20,000, roughly, implying a total cost of $1 billion.

WEAPONS ACQUISITION REFORM

In 2008 a Government Accountability Office (GAO) study examining ninety-five major military weapons acquisition programs found projected cost overruns of $295 billion (see table 4-3, figure 4-1). A subsequent update the next year found that figure essentially unchanged. Although cost overruns are hardly news at the Pentagon, this GAO estimate stands in contrast to a figure of $202 billion just two years earlier—and of just $42 billion in 2000. In addition, the number of programs showing 25 percent or more cost growth relative to initial projections grew from 37 percent of major programs in 2000 to 44 percent of late.[28]

Some key programs, such as the Navy's littoral combat ship, are in jeopardy of being canceled, since at some point high cost may defeat their very purpose. For example, this ship, known as LCS, was designed to be economical enough that the Navy could afford fairly large numbers of them—without that benefit, the very rationale of the program is called into doubt. These disturbing realities raise a number of pertinent issues, many of them addressed previously in earlier eras of defense reform—but obviously with imperfect results:

TABLE 4-3. Selected Acquisition Report Program Acquisition Cost Summary[a]

(as of September 30, 2008, in millions of dollars)

Weapons system	Base year	Current estimate Base year dollars	Current dollars	Quantity
Army				
Apache Block III (AB3)	2006	7,158	8,996	639
ARH	2005	502	537	—
ATIRCM/CMWS	2003	4,170	4,816	3,589
Black Hawk upgrade	2005	18,935	24,043	1,235
Bradley upgrade	2001	8,570	9,695	2,568
CH-47F	2005	11,516	13,350	513
Excalibur	2007	2,233	2,465	30,388
FBCB2	2005	3,545	3,729	80,418
FCS	2003	112,425	159,320	15
FMTV	1996	16,517	20,676	83,185
GMLRS	2003	4,718	6,008	43,795
HIMARS	2003	1,797	2,049	381
JCA	2007	3,635	4,088	78
JLENS	2005	6,089	7,500	16
Longbow Apache	1996	9,826	11,183	671
LUH	2006	1,820	2,090	345
Patriot PAC-3	2002	8,387	8,525	969
Patriot/MEADS CAP- Fire Unit	2004	15,808	21,780	48
Patriot/MEADS CAP- Missile	2004	6,027	8,116	1,528
Stryker	2004	14,255	15,691	3,537
WIN-T increment 1	2007	3,798	3,860	1,677
WIN-T increment 2	2007	3,446	3,871	1,893
Subtotal, Army		265,174	342,388	
Navy				
AGM-88E AARGM	2003	1,426	1,710	1,911
AIM-9X	1997	2,664	3,396	10,142
CEC	2002	4,207	4,531	306
CH-53K	2006	15,025	18,708	156
Cobra Judy replacement	2003	1,453	1,630	1
CVN 21	2000	24,987	35,119	3
CVN 68	1995	5,279	6,259	1
DDG 1000	2005	25,090	28,887	7
DDG 51	1987	46,418	62,756	62
E-2D AHE	2002	13,394	17,431	75
EA-18G	2004	7,578	8,649	85

Weapons system	Base year	Current estimate		Quantity
		Base year dollars	Current dollars	
EA-6B ICAP III	2008	1,130	1,054	32
EFV	2007	13,164	15,860	593
F/A-18 E/F	2000	43,258	46,345	493
H-1 upgrades (4BW/4BN)	1996	6,750	8,728	284
IDECM-Block 2/3	2008	1,411	1,535	12,809
IDECM-Block 4	2008	661	746	160
Joint MRAP	2008	22,014	22,415	15,374
JSOW- Baseline/BLU-108	1990	1,476	1,862	3,334
JSOW- Unitary	1990	1,777	2,725	7,000
LCS	2004	2,595	2,849	2
LHA replacement	2006	3,079	3,368	1
LPD 17	1996	11,508	14,242	9
MH-60R	2006	11,279	12,139	254
MH-60S	1998	6,504	7,843	271
MUOS	2004	5,667	6,682	6
NMT	2002	1,677	2,103	305
P-8A (MMA)	2004	26,183	32,853	113
RMS	2006	1,380	1,550	108
SM-6	2004	4,693	5,954	1,200
SSN 774 (Virginia Class)	1995	63,752	91,965	30
Tactical Tomahawk	1999	3,706	4,375	3,292
T-AKE	2000	4,618	5,715	12
Trident II missile	1983	26,382	38,817	561
V-22	2005	50,473	54,227	458
VH-71	2003	5,732	6,750	28
VTUAV	2006	1,875	2,158	177
Subtotal, Navy		470,265	583,935	
Air Force				
AEHF	2002	8,841	9,939	4
AMRAAM	1992	13,156	14,881	13,953
B-2 EHF increment I	2007	636	681	21
B-2 RMP	2004	1,094	1,225	21
C-130 AMP	2000	4,521	5,800	222
C-130J	1996	9,805	12,029	134
C-17A	1996	58,665	62,307	190
C-5 AMP	2006	1,377	1,405	112

(continued)

TABLE 4-3 (*continued*)

| | | Current estimate | | |
Weapons system	Base year	Base year dollars	Current dollars	Quantity
C-5 RERP	2000	7,147	7,694	52
F-22	2005	66,992	64,540	184
FAB-T	2002	2,963	3,622	222
GBS	1997	727	806	1,121
Global Hawk (RQ-4A/B)	2000	8,102	9,741	54
GPS IIIA	2000	3,180	4,002	8
JASSM	1995	4,466	6,066	5,006
JDAM	1995	4,522	5,260	201,993
JPATS	2002	4,915	5,534	768
LAIRCM	2008	384	366	8
Minuteman III PRP	1994	2,190	2,602	601
MP RTIP	2000	1,115	1,225	—
NAS	2005	1,424	1,491	91
NAVSTAR GPS- Space & Control	2000	5,963	6,306	33
NAVSTAR GPS- User Equipment	2000	1,791	2,094	—
NPOESS	2002	9,363	11,140	4
SBIRS High	1995	9,559	11,555	4
SBSS B10	2007	811	824	1
SDB I	2001	1,252	1,477	24,070
WGS	2001	1,764	1,951	5
Subtotal, Air Force		236,722	256,561	
DoD				
BMDS	2002	89,398	102,912	—
CHEM DEMIL- ACWA	1994	5,499	7,992	3,136
CHEM DEMIL- CMA	1994	22,459	27,423	29,060
F-35 (JSF)	2002	210,015	298,843	2,456
JTRS GMR	2002	14,243	20,536	86,652
JTRS HMS	2004	2,672	3,367	95,961
JTRS NED	2002	1,743	1,962	—
MIDS	2003	2,289	2,373	3,807
Subtotal, DoD		348,318	465,408	
Grand total		1,320,477	1,648,292	

Source: Department of Defense, "SAR Program Acquisition Cost Summary" table (www. defenselink.mil/news/SAR%20Acquisition%20Cost%20Table%20(2).pdf).

a. Totals may not add because of rounding. Each weapon is assigned a base year based on key milestones in its development; costs as expressed in "base year dollars" are measured in that base year's constant dollars. All procurement as well as research, development, test, and evaluation costs are included. Actual costs can, of course, grow even more.

FIGURE 4-1. Department of Defense Annual Budget Authority for Procurement, FY 1948–2013[a]

Billions of dollars

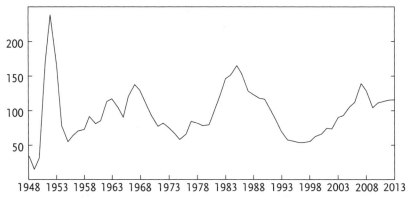

Source: U.S. Department of Defense, *National Defense Budget Estimates for FY 2009* (Washington, March 2008), pp. 103–08.
a. Includes supplementals. Amounts are in constant FY 2009 dollars.

—Why do today's weapons cost so much more than earlier generations of weapons—and why do projections of a given weapon's costs seem to be rising so fast in so many cases?

—Is the Pentagon's aging weapons acquisition workforce losing its touch? And who will replace those who are now retiring in large numbers?

Naturally, weapons cost more as they improve, explaining why one fighter jet or ship tends to cost much more than its predecessor. And the fact that some cost growth occurs in a given weapons program, as it advances from early R&D to engineering development to production, is hardly surprising either. After all, developing new weapons means inventing new technologies and systems, and the process of invention is hard to set to a schedule or a strict budget. That said, defense contractors cannot be allowed to gold-plate weapons with impunity or become so sloppy in their bookkeeping or other work that costs go up inordinately.

One set of solutions is to structure contracts so that industry has an incentive to look for economies where possible. For example, rather than awarding a *cost plus* contract that simply adds a fixed percentage to documented costs as a profit margin (thereby rewarding companies for making weapons more expensive), it makes sense to create incentives for weapons costs to be lower, by tying some or all of a profit margin to producing a weapon at lower cost. This is not always feasible in a given instance but is worth attempting in some cases.

It is also important that there be discipline—and good judgment—in deciding which weapons to buy. Procedural reform can help to a degree. For example, the idea of Clark Murdoch and other authors of the Beyond Goldwater-Nichols study project, as well as the Defense Business Board, to have combatant commands play a greater role in validating weapons needs of the services makes sense. As one possible improved approach, the deputy combatant commanders might replace the deputy service chiefs on the so-called Joint Requirements Oversight Council, or JROC.[29]

In general, weapons specifications should not change as the weapons are being developed and built either; this is a recipe for cost growth. It is also important to develop fairly robust designs of weapons, using demonstrated component technologies, before approving full-scale development and production of key weaponry. GAO found that, of the programs it examined that had shifting specifications, costs increased 72 percent (in contrast to just 11 percent for systems with clear performance requirements that remained consistent). Moreover, for those systems involving immature technologies, development costs grew 44 percent more than for those employing established component technologies. (Sometimes urgent circumstances may require developing a weapon even as some of its technologies remain in major flux, but this can and should be avoided in general.)[30] A related problem is contractors overpromising on the affordability of weapons even when fully aware of the immaturity of many component technologies; this tendency gave raise to a serious idea by Senator Carl Levin to consider creating an independent director of cost assessments at the Pentagon with authority to reach meaningful decisions about when contractors were failing to be adequately transparent in their predictions of future cost.[31]

There is another real concern with current contracting: the state of the military acquisition workforce. A great deal has been outsourced in recent years; Secretary Gates wishes to reverse that trend, reducing contracting jobs by nearly 40,000 in the coming years (about half of that related to defense acquisitions).[32] Much of the workforce is nearing retirement age, and there is worry that it is not being replaced with younger individuals of comparable commitment or ability.[33] In theory, younger workers could gain the experience and knowledge with time—

but today's U.S. economy does not create a culture in which individuals typically stay with their jobs as long as they once did. As such, there is real worry about the future of the acquisition workforce. Even today, there are problems; GAO recently found that since 2001 the average tenure in a job for program managers was just 17 months, or less than half what official DoD policy suggests.[34]

To counter this, new programs are needed to foster several trends:

—To encourage more top-notch young professionals to work for DoD in acquisition force jobs

—To encourage mid-career professionals to consider joining DoD, for short stints or longer stints

—To create better public-private partnerships, so that some oversight can be provided by private firms at the same time that DoD retains a meaningful oversight capacity

No simple fix-all policy option is available to address these concerns, and they are hardly unique to the DoD acquisition workforce. But a number of concepts should be applied to the problem:

—A scholarship program should be set up for those willing to commit to several years of government service. Such a program should be competitive and generous to have the maximum effect, with substantial stipends for graduate study in particular for a modest number of highly skilled individuals.

—There has to be careful development of conflict-of-interest regulations that, while preventing future "Darlene Druyun" scandals (military officials rewarding a company with a major contract that then offers the individuals employment) as much as possible, do not discourage talented people from considering government service. In particular, asking individuals to recuse themselves from decisions involving previous companies and maintaining a relatively modest period between the end of government service and when a person is eligible to begin private employment with a relevant company (such as one year, the current approach) probably amounts to roughly the right mix of policies.

—Finally, while science and technology budgets have been robust in the Department of Defense since the end of the cold war, holding steady at inflation-adjusted Reagan-era levels through the 1990s and then increasing by about a third in this decade, there are some reasons for worry about the long-term health of the United States' science capabilities.[35] Many of these arise from trends in advanced science degrees, patents, and publications around the world; the United States is simply less dominant in science than before and has fewer students pursuing scientific pursuits than in the past. These trend lines require further attention and greater resources for scholarship programs, whether funded through DoD or (better yet) elsewhere in the government.[36] A total of $750 million a year is recommended for these various scholarship programs, which could provide about 20,000 people with generous levels of support.

Aircraft

While awaiting reforms in the acquisition process to take effect, it is important to find ways to save money from existing programs as well. A good place to start is with modernization programs for manned combat aircraft, which remain extremely expensive even as the United States enjoys overwhelming military dominance in the air today. The Air Force, however, argues that at least in terms of the maximal capabilities of respective aircraft (leaving aside quality and training of pilots, as well as the command and control and communications networks linking planes together in a fighting force), foreign systems such as the Russian Su-30 and even the Chinese F-11B now surpass U.S. aircraft such as the F-14, F-15, and F-16.[37]

The U.S. Air Force, before the firing of its chief of staff and top civilian by Secretary of Defense Robert Gates in the spring of 2008, complained about a shortfall of $20 billion in its annual budget, largely due to its perceived need to buy more fighter aircraft in the coming years. At one level, the Air Force was right. The plans that it has on the books—plans that have been blessed by several successive administrations in one way or another—call for replacing essentially all of its 20 tactical combat wings with "fifth generation" aircraft that restore clear and categorical dominance to U.S. combat aircraft. (See the appendix for current inventories and ages of active duty aircraft.) Since a wing typically includes close to 100 planes, when extra aircraft for the maintenance pipeline and attrition reserve and so forth are included, and since those next-generation aircraft (the F-22 Raptor and F-35 Lightning II) are estimated to cost on average at least $150 million and $95 million, respectively, by CBO and GAO, costs are naturally very high. The total estimated price tags for the F-22 and F-35 programs (the latter also involving the Navy and Marine Corps) are nearly $70 billion and $275 billion, respectively, including research and development costs.[38] Then there are all the other Air Force costs ranging from unmanned aircraft to tanker and transport planes to reconnaissance assets—not to mention ongoing costs of operations and people. There is little reason to doubt the math of those officials calling for more funds.

But there are ample grounds to doubt, and question, the plans undergirding those budgetary projections. The Air Force's arithmetic may be accurate, but its assessment of what it needs to protect the nation in the coming years is excessively expensive, especially since it will certainly have a far stronger aircraft fleet than any other country even if not all of its planes are fifth-generation models. In addition, it has not adequately recognized the value of all the new capabilities that modern technology provides it, ranging from the greater precision of modern munitions to the capabilities of UAVs to the increased benefits per aircraft produced by stealthy jets—to the new aerial assets now possessed by the other military services as well.

Throughout much of the post–cold war era, defense reformers and budget hawks counseled the Air Force to reconsider its modernization plans. Experts like Lane Pierrot (formerly at CBO), Chuck Spinney within the Pentagon, and numerous think tank specialists have suggested that buying a force made up entirely of F-22s and F-35s was too expensive. As usual, the Air Force tried to justify its appetite with very cautious assessments of what the future war fighting environment would be like, very traditional views about the future of manned aircraft in that environment, and very optimistic perspectives on how much it would all cost. It is always tempting to assume that next-generation systems will somehow be not only better but cheaper, or at least no more expensive, than their predecessors. And when new aircraft are to be built using new procedures or new materials, it is difficult for independent auditors and other experts to challenge such optimism even when most realize that it is probably unwarranted.

Critics have called for cheaper approaches, like buying new F-16 aircraft with modern avionics and stealthy coatings that could reduce its radar cross section by at least half (even if not by the 90 percent or more that an F-35 might provide). Such approaches would be more than adequate for fighting the likes of Milosevic's Serbia and Saddam's Iraq. Even against more capable foes, they could handle follow-on waves of attacks against less defended targets while the stealthiest aircraft were used against the most difficult and dangerous aimpoints. Critics have also pointed out that buying planes like the F-16 could be done quickly, mitigating the problems of an aging aircraft fleet.[39]

The most logical idea now is not to cancel the aircraft programs, but to seriously reassess the numbers of F-35 aircraft intended for purchase. In an era when so much more is being done by smart munitions delivered from considerable distance, and from unmanned aerial vehicles, a traditionally sized and scaled fighter modernization program is not appropriate. At currently intended levels, the F-35 program will cost an average of about $14 billion a year through 2023 and $10 billion a year for several years thereafter. Moreover, the program is being rushed into production. At the start of low-rate production, for example, the F-35 had gone through only three months of flight testing and less than 1 percent of all intended flight test hours, in contrast to figures of forty-eight months and 20 percent for the F-22, for example.[40] This is not a suggestion for a long postponement of the program. Not only the United States, but a total of nine foreign partners await the aircraft and are counting on it already, with a number of significant financial contributors to the F-35's development.[41] But a bit more care, and less haste, makes sense.

There are two main ways the program could be scaled back. First, the Air Force, Navy, and Marine Corps could keep their force structure but reduce the number of F-35s and increase the number of F-16-vintage planes instead. Rather than have a combined total of about twenty-five tactical combat wings with F-35 aircraft, they could instead have fifteen, and then outfit the remaining ten with F-16 or F-18 class aircraft and some armed UAVs to save money. The typical previous-generation plane would, on average, cost about $35 million less to build at this point than the corresponding variant of the F-35, so even accounting for a somewhat higher cost of Joint Strike Fighter (JSF) planes when bought in smaller quantities, savings for adopting this approach would be $25 billion or more.[42] Re-winging existing planes might be viable in many cases too; a plan for the A-10 jet is to double expected flying lifetime at a cost of less than $5 million a plane (though admittedly the situation may be somewhat different for higher-performance aircraft).[43]

A second option would be to scale back the number of manned combat aircraft wings but outfit all of them with state-of-the-art aircraft. In other words, the services could choose to emphasize either quantity or quality, but not both, at least not to the planned degree.

As a matter of practical policymaking, the best choice might be to let the Air Force itself decide—that is, within budget constraints on tactical combat aircraft set by civilian leadership that ensured that the Air Force would properly pursue other types of capabilities (such as unmanned systems, transport and refueling capabilities, and reconnaissance and intelligence assets). In fact, it could even be granted leeway to buy more F-22s as long as it found the means to pay for this very expensive fighter—without the added $20 billion a year in funding that it was requesting in recent years. Regardless, the Air Force should be asked to make near-term decisions in a way that would be difficult to reverse later. Either its force structure should be reduced promptly or its purchases of new F-16s should be accelerated (to lock it into maintaining such aircraft over the longer term), depending on the option chosen.

A brief word is in order as well on refueling aircraft. They are needed for lift, for bombers, and for fighters and as such are crucial to U.S. global operations. As of this writing, the renewed competition between Boeing and a consortium of Northrop Grumman and European Aeronautic Defence and Space Company (EADS) has been deferred, after the latter consortium won the original competition (which was later challenged). The main point is that this program needs to be pursued soon. While there are other options for some refueling aircraft, including refurbishing existing planes and converting existing commercial planes into tankers, the deferred competition is for only a modest fraction of the Air Force's overall tanking needs, and the existing fleet is decades old. The idea of a split buy, as proposed by some as a political compromise, may be tolerable if necessary. But it does not seem optimal for a type of technology that in the end is not among the most advanced or original; preserving competition in the supplier base for such a product is less crucial than for state-of-the-art capabilities such as fighter jets. The key point, again, is to get on with this matter and avoid exacerbating an increasingly serious problem across much of the U.S. military—excessively old equipment.[44]

Brief mention is also warranted for the Marine Corps V-22 Osprey aircraft. This tilt-rotor aircraft is faster and has a longer range than helicopters, but it is also much more expensive—yet not particularly more survivable when flying slowly during takeoffs and landings. It has utility for certain types of missions, like special operations that require speed and range and relative stealth, but it is too expensive to be worth the money as the workhorse for an amphibious lift operation. Such operations are unlikely in any event and are further constrained by the difficulties of surmounting sea mines planted by a prepared enemy. These types of operations also require helicopters for cargo transport regardless of whether V-22 aircraft are available. If these operations do become necessary, most of the agility for carrying them out is provided by the amphibious ships themselves, not the shorter-range aircraft (or amphibious vehicles) now being pursued in large numbers and at high expense. Scaling back the program to roughly 100 aircraft for the Marine Corps, Air Force, and Special Operations command and purchasing large helicopters instead of buying the other 360 V-22 aircraft could save $10 billion, or nearly $1 billion a year.[45]

Secretary Gates has also advocated canceling the VH-71 helicopter for use by the president and other top officials, a program intended to replace the VH-3D and VH-60N, alas at a cost of $13 billion. This price tag is rather exorbitant for some twenty-eight aircraft. A more modest program could save $10 billion.

Army Acquisition Strategy

Since the distinguished tenure of General Eric Shinseki as chief of staff, the U.S. Army has been committed to a broad-based modernization of its entire force structure known as the Future Combat System. Originally conceived as a family of eighteen major systems—eleven ground vehicles, four unmanned aerial vehicles, and three other major capabilities—it has since been scaled back to fourteen systems. The original cost was to be less than $100 billion, as projected in 2003, but estimated costs running through 2025 are now independently estimated at $200 billion or more in constant 2009 dollars. The goal of FCS has been to use information, networks, situational awareness, active defenses, and maneuver rather than heavy-armored protection as the key means of ensuring survivability.

The FCS concept is too ambitious. Pursuing so many capabilities at once risks confusion. It has proven too rushed in a number of technology areas.[46] It ignores the fact that often, in the age of advanced computing and electronics, add-on capabilities are cheaper and nearly as effective as creating whole new vehicle fleets from scratch. Moreover, the Army is already adding lots of new vehicles to its fleet this decade, including several thousand medium-weight wheeled "Strykers" and up

CONVENTIONAL MILITARY FORCES AND OPERATIONS **87**

to 15,000 mine-resistant ambush-protected vehicles (10,000 had been built by mid-2008, with more than 5,000 deployed to Iraq and almost 1,000 to Afghanistan by that point). These should be used and analyzed and evaluated before major new decisions are made.[47]

If FCS is too ambitious in some ways, it has proven insufficiently flexible as a program over the last decade as well. It has not evolved sufficiently as a result of lessons learned from the Iraq and Afghanistan experiences. For most of the decade, it continued to feature an infantry vehicle with a low, flat bottom rather than a V-shaped hull of the type that has protected soldiers and marines so well in MRAPs. In addition, to the extent lessons from Iraq and Afghanistan have been learned, much of the result has been to add armor, and weight, to chassis designed for much lighter loads. This fact casts doubt about the future reliability of any FCS vehicles.

Rather than pursue the FCS program as currently conceived, the Army should distinguish between sensors, munitions, and communications on the one hand and vehicles on the other. It should pursue the former while canceling the latter, instead refurbishing existing vehicles for the foreseeable future. An individual vehicle here or there could be restored to the development or production line as deemed appropriate, but as individually managed and more modest efforts rather than sweeping modernization agendas.

Taking this approach would, according to the Congressional Budget Office, leave the Army with a residual cost of about $100 billion through 2025 rather than the otherwise likely $200 billion or more.[48] Savings would not be as great if a key vehicle or two was in the end retained, but they should still reach or exceed $4 billion a year.

NAVY ACQUISITION STRATEGY

Although it was U.S. Air Force leadership that incurred the wrath of Secretary of Defense Robert Gates in 2008, the Navy's problems are at least as severe, at least in the realm of weapons acquisition. It also faces the challenge of buying the F-35 aircraft—and then its problems continue. Of its various shipbuilding efforts, at least two have been seriously troubled to the point of leading to cancellations of contracts—for the small littoral combat ship (LCS) and the technologically complex DDG-1000 destroyer ship, the latter of which Gates now wants to terminate (and instead resume construction of more DDG-51 destroyers).[49] Rather than relying on two troubled new programs in its surface fleet, the Navy is reverting to an old workhorse in the form of the DDG-51 while still holding out hope for the LCS.[50] However, that LCS program is clearly in trouble; it may now cost $500 million per ship—more than twice what was originally predicted.[51]

Beyond the specific problems with individual programs, as bad as they are, is a huge structural budgetary problem: The Navy has been buying ships at a slow pace in recent years, and to make up for that, it will need to increase its annual shipbuilding budget by as much as $15 billion if its plans are to be fulfilled—a shortfall not unlike the Air Force's purported recent $20 billion annual funding gap.[52]

But just as there are ways to rethink Air Force acquisition strategies, there are ways to do the same for the Navy as well. Its plan as unveiled in 2006 is to have a fleet of about 314 warships, somewhat larger than its fleet today of 280 ships. That fleet of 314 ships would include 14 ballistic missile submarines as part of the nuclear weapons force, 4 cruise missile submarines (presently former ballistic missile submarines), 48 attack submarines, 12 aircraft carriers, 88 large surface combatants (cruisers, destroyers, and frigates), 55 (or more) small warships known as littoral combat ships, 31 amphibious ships, 12 maritime prepositioning ships, 30 combat resupply logistics ships, and 20 other vessels including command ships.[53] To reach that goal, over the next thirty years the Navy intends to build roughly seven aircraft carriers, sixty-five large surface combatants, fifty-five littoral combat ships, forty-eight attack subs, twelve ballistic missile submarines, twenty amphibious ships, nine maritime prepositioning ships, and fifty-two support ships.[54]

The above section on nuclear weapons suggested reducing the ballistic missile submarine fleet by eight vessels, to a total of six ships, and the following section on overseas military basing suggests a way to further reduce the attack submarine fleet by eight ships as well. It also suggests a way to reduce the size of the aircraft carrier fleet by one ship and associated escort vessels. Those savings are not double-counted here, but to note again, over a thirty-year period, the average annual savings would be at least $2 billion for the submarine reductions and again as much for the carrier cutback.[55]

The Navy can go even further. While it is to be commended for introducing new concepts of late, including a less expensive and smaller ship in the LCS (with a crew of 75 instead of 200 to 300, which is more usual for warships, and displacement of about 3,000 tons, less than half what is common), it has failed to execute that program well, and its ideas of having a larger fleet in the future seem unnecessary.

To be sure, China and other powers are becoming stronger and in some cases building larger navies. Iran remains a major worry in the strategically crucial Persian Gulf as well, and there are various scenarios that could lead to protracted naval operations against Iran including possible blockades.[56] Police actions are also possible against threats such as Somali pirates.[57]

Rather than get bigger, the Navy should continue to get smarter in how it uses its fleet. It has been innovative in recent years and deserves credit. For example, it has moved to a strategy of surging ships to key theaters overseas rather than consistently maintaining a constant, predictable, constraining presence in each. This allows more flexibility and places fewer slavish demands on the fleet (thereby also allowing a comparable number of missions to be successfully conducted by somewhat fewer ships). But the Navy can also go further with the idea of having two crews per ship. To date this has been used with submarines and mine warfare ships and a couple of other specialty vessels. It could in theory be used with larger ships, and in fact Navy experiments along these lines have worked well in general. (With this approach, the Navy flies crews back and forth from the United States to the Western Pacific, or Persian Gulf region—obviating the need for long, slow ocean transits of vessels.)[58] The Navy should be able to hold the line on fleet size with the gradual introduction of such measures. In addition to the submarine savings noted before, this translates into one fewer ship built per year, saving on average $1 billion a piece (since some are LCSs, others the more expensive DDG-51s).[59] Savings on operating costs are partially canceled out by the need for two crews per ship, but two-thirds of the savings can still be accrued. Taking those as about $100 million a ship a year, this translates into a total of $1.1 billion annually in savings, beyond those from the smaller submarine fleets.

Two other ideas can reduce Navy procurement budgets (although no savings are assumed here, as the ideas are preliminary in nature). First, more ships can be kept in the fleet for forty years or more, rather than replaced at roughly the thirty-year mark. Since aircraft carriers are often operated up to half a century, it is not clear why other vessels cannot be. Second, some new types of ships such as M Ship Company's innovative

Stiletto could be considered, which costs less than $10 million a ship and emphasizes stealthy operations through a wake-capture mechanism in its hull and small superstructure and other means. It is especially promising as an alternative to some LCS ships.[60]

Since Marine Corps budgets are within those of the Department of the Navy, a further word is necessary to discuss one more Marine Corps acquisition program: the Expeditionary Fighting Vehicle. The vehicle, designed to be much faster than current variants, has grown enormously in cost, to nearly $25 million a vehicle. It is very dubious that amphibious assault requirements necessitate such a vehicle, for the same kinds of reasons discussed above in regard to the V-22. There is a strong case to purchase a more modest amphibious vehicle, such as a South Korean variant, and to save the lion's share of funding envisioned over the next half dozen years for this planned $10 billion program for the Expeditionary Fighting Vehicle.[61]

OVERSEAS MILITARY BASING

The Rumsfeld era at the Department of Defense will undoubtedly be most remembered for the Iraq war, and beyond that, for the U.S. response to 9/11 including the overthrow of the Taliban in Afghanistan. It is only natural that a secretary of defense find his place in history first and foremost for the wars fought on his watch. But another central element of Rumsfeld's legacy is the way in which he reshaped America's global military base network.[62] Realigning bases also has budgetary implications, less because of the effects on force structure, which tend to be modest, and more because of the expenses involved in building new facilities at home or abroad as forces are shifted about.

Recent base realignments have been occurring through a process that began shortly after 9/11 and that continues today. The process was formally codified as the Integrated Global Presence and Basing Strategy (IGPBS), though for simplicity it will be referred to here as the Global Posture Review, or GPR. A vocal advocate of military transformation, Rumsfeld probably did as much to reshape the U.S. armed forces through the GPR as through his changes to policies on weapons modernization, force structure, military personnel, or any other major aspect of defense policy. It is no mean feat to change global basing arrangements; as Kent Calder has argued, once established, they tend to display considerable inertia and prove difficult to modify.[63] Fortunately, Rumsfeld's record with the GPR is likely to be more positive than his war fighting legacy—though it will take additional work and effort on the part of the Obama administration to fix several problems with existing plans and thereby ensure this.

The September 2004 GPR report to Congress states the GPR's goals as "to assure allies, dissuade potential challengers, deter our enemies, and defeat aggression if necessary." These echo the core national security objectives of the Bush administration's earlier Quadrennial Defense Review of 2001.[64] (The 2004 goals do not repeat the preemption language of the 2002 National Security Strategy, though they are consistent with other goals and principles of that controversial document.[65]) Indeed, they echo much of the underlying bipartisan philosophy behind U.S. foreign policy throughout the last several decades.

The GPR report focuses on three overall types of threats: "the nexus among terrorism, state sponsors of terrorism, and proliferation of weapons of mass destruction; ungoverned states and under-governed areas within states, which can serve as both a breeding ground and a sanctuary for terrorists and other transnational threats; and potential adversaries' adoption of asymmetric approaches—including irregular warfare, weapons of mass destruction, and advanced, disruptive, technological challenges—designed to counter U.S. conventional military superiority."[66] Its logic is reinforced in the subsequent 2006 Quadrennial Defense Review, which lays out several relevant DoD goals: "having the authorities and resources to build partnership capacity, achieve unity of effort, and adopt indirect approaches to act with and through others to defeat common enemies . . . shifting from responsive actions toward early, preventive measures and increasing the speed of action to stop problems from becoming conflicts or crises . . . increasing the freedom of action of the United States and its allies and partners in meeting the security challenges of the 21st century."[67] These are generally reasonable criteria. As such it makes sense to evaluate the GPR largely against these standards.

The GPR encompasses everything from the creation of new bases in Central Asia and Eastern Europe to the downsizing of the U.S. military presence in Germany to a reduction and realignment of the U.S. presence in South Korea as well as Okinawa, Japan. These changes are designed to improve U.S. and allied options for handling new developments—such as the ongoing struggle against extremism and terrorism, the rise of China, and enduring problems such as the North Korean and Iranian regimes. Of course, there have also been enormous changes in the Persian Gulf, the largest related to ongoing operations in Iraq, and the subsequent elimination of U.S. combat forces from Saudi Arabia and Turkey. (Deployment patterns of naval vessels have also changed a good deal, but the base infrastructure supporting them has changed less in recent years.)

According to the plan, about 70,000 U.S. military personnel are to return to the United States over a ten-year implementation period. These figures do not count any additional reductions from the Iraq and Afghanistan operations over the same time period. Another 100,000 Americans who are either civilian employees of DoD or family members of the troops coming home will return stateside as well. The 70,000 troops slated for return represent just under 30 percent of the 250,000 personnel the United States deployed abroad before 9/11, although less than 20 percent of the total that were deployed when the review was announced in 2004 (with the Iraq and Afghanistan operations fully under way). The total number of U.S. military sites abroad is declining from 850 to 550 over that same ten-year period of drawdown (not counting sites in Iraq or Afghanistan).[68] That 35 percent cut in the number of facilities will translate into a reduction of somewhat more than 20 percent of the total value of the assets used by U.S. forces abroad, which topped $100 billion earlier this decade.[69]

Under the new plan, of the 70,000 troops slated to come home, about 15,000 were initially in Asia.[70] The reductions there are occurring largely through consolidation of redundant headquarters in Korea and Japan and a reduction of Army combat capability in Korea from two brigades to one (in fact, the latter change has already occurred). In Europe, while some streamlining is occurring in Air Force and Navy assets, most changes are in the Army. The total number of soldiers will decline from 62,000 to 28,000, if original 2004 plans hold, with most of those leaving eventually relocating to U.S. facilities such as Fort Riley in Kansas and Fort Bliss in Texas.[71]

The GPR is not solely a force drawdown. In addition to presumably temporary deployments in Iraq and Afghanistan, there are a number of other places where U.S. capabilities and even troop totals are being augmented. These include parts of Japan, Guam, Romania, Bulgaria, and Central Asia. The GPR also builds on less trumpeted but still important strengthening of the United States posture in the 1990s in places such as the smaller Persian Gulf nations and Diego Garcia in the Indian Ocean.

In terms of specific threats and opportunities, the GPR focused in the first instance largely on the global war on terror. But its catalysts, and its objectives, run deeper. Specifically, it was also motivated by shifting power balances among major states, most notably the rise of the People's Republic of China (PRC). Some analysts have argued that China's rise could not plausibly lead to great-power rivalry. However, the GPR did not endorse this view.[72] It is not clear to what extent the Pentagon views China's rise as a general matter of likely hegemonic competition among great powers with broad ramifications and to what extent it is the specific unsettled issue of Taiwan that most concerns the Pentagon. Regardless, the motivation for changes in Japan, Guam, and even Korea is largely to hedge against the possibility of future difficulty with the PRC. The aggregate changes are not excessive, given that overall U.S. force totals in the region are actually decreasing modestly. But reductions in U.S. ground forces in Korea, focused almost exclusively on the defense of South Korea (ROK), are being juxtaposed with increases in submarine and aircraft capabilities on Guam.[73] In addition, plans to relocate some of the Okinawa-based marines from that island to Guam will have no net effect on the United States' overall Marine Corps presence in the Western Pacific, while presumably shoring up Japan's willingness to keep crucial U.S. Air Force assets on Okinawa.

It is worth noting that none of these types of facilities are needed for the small-scale training and operational partnerships emphasized by the Bush administration as part of its way of fighting the long-term war against extremism. Such activities do not require highly visible sites where Americans are based.[74] Generally, trainers are better off operating out of embassies, or private locations, or even indigenous bases operated by indigenous forces—not out of declared, distinctive U.S. facilities. There can be exceptions to this generalization, of course, in places where there is a great deal of United States–led training, for example, or in places where the host nation truly wants a visible U.S. presence.[75] But for the most part, such activities do not have great bearing on the United States' global base network.

What are the financial implications of overseas bases? The budgetary costs of the GPR, including construction costs for new or expanding bases (and shutdown and cleanup costs for older ones) are estimated to range from $9 billion to $12 billion for initial investment according to DoD.[76] However, the congressionally mandated Overseas Basing Commission offered an estimate of $20 billion in its 2005 report.[77]

These are real sums of money. But the budgetary importance of overseas basing decisions is often less than many assume. For one thing, the costs of routinely rotating people around are modest—typically in the hundreds of millions of dollars a year for forces numbering in the range of tens of thousands, for example.[78] The costs to DoD of maintaining schools overseas for military dependents are nontrivial, of course, but again, the annual expenses for tens of thousands of military families abroad total in the hundreds of millions of dollars—not the many billions. And foreign bases in the right place can save substantial sums of money. For example, being able to base U.S. tactical airpower at Kadena Air Base on Okinawa, Japan, arguably saves the United States several billion dollars a year, since the alternative to Kadena might well be a larger Navy aircraft carrier fleet expanded by three or four carrier battle groups.[79]

There is an important caveat in regard to finances, however. There are always real one-time costs associated with building new bases and relocating forces that if incurred quickly can make for big yearly price tags. Moving 8,000 marines from Okinawa to Guam is expected to cost up to $15 billion. And with the post–cold war defense downsizing process complete, as well as most surplus bases now identified and closed, there will not be enough facilities at which to relocate Army soldiers returning from Germany and Korea in short order. This is especially true in light of the ongoing increase in the size of the active Army, announced after the GPR was complete (with an overall increase of roughly 65,000 soldiers now expected). As discussed subsequently, therefore, it would not be at all surprising if plans for reductions in U.S. troops in Europe were slowed or even modified in the coming years. Indeed, to some extent this is already happening.

The Global Posture Review is on balance good policy. The drawdown and consolidation in Europe do not deliver huge dividends, but they do deliver modest and useful ones. They help consolidate the U.S. Army in particular at a smaller number of bases, which should over time improve the quality of life for soldiers and their families. New capabilities in Romania and Bulgaria keep the alliance vibrant and forward-looking. Leaving aside the major exceptions of Iraq and Afghanistan, additional capabilities in the broader Mideast–Central Asia region are being developed gradually and moderately, in keeping with the fact that most U.S. partners in those regions do not share America's interests and values to quite the degree traditional allies in Europe and East Asia do. Streamlining U.S. forces in Korea and moving those that remain southward is consistent with realities on the peninsula—a continually improving ROK military, as well as dense population concentrations in and around Seoul (as well as the need for more U.S. forces elsewhere in the world). Reduction of the U.S. Marine Corps presence on Okinawa should alleviate a political problem for Tokyo; beefing up military capabilities on Guam, by contrast, takes advantage of good opportunities and convenient geography, and helps hedge against the possibility of future rivalry with China (while also positioning assets reasonably well for possible scenarios in Southeast Asia, South Asia, or the Persian Gulf).

The following pages offer several suggestions about how policymakers might modify or adapt the strategy to improve its strengths and mitigate its few but still important current failings in the years ahead. The budgetary implications, relative to the GPR's own plans and projections, allow some additional savings. As noted below, adding more attack submarines to Guam (while perhaps reducing modestly the size of the fleet) could save a billion dollars a year. So could the notion of keeping a couple more Army brigades in Europe than currently planned (since facilities exist in Europe that would have to be built in the States). Cutting an aircraft carrier out of the force posture, by virtue of forward-deploying another to the Pacific, would add substantial savings if possible. The main additional costs projected below are less than these savings. They involve hardening bases on locations such as Guam against possible attack, adding the port infrastructure to base an additional aircraft carrier in the Pacific region, and over time gradually (and modestly) expanding military facilities in Africa. Each of these ideas would typically add $100 million to $200 million a year in costs to the United States for the coming years (although a serious hardening program could keep added costs at that level indefinitely).

THE NAVY, GUAM, AND OTHER OPPORTUNITIES

The Navy's ongoing moves toward a greater dispersal of assets abroad are smart policy and should continue. It is also wise to have made its overseas ship deployments more flexible, with ship journeys more a function of global opportunities as well as crises and less strictly tied to the dictates of a calendar. Most notable to date, in addition to the new and more flexible fleet response program for maintaining forward naval deployments, has been the introduction of attack submarines to basing on Guam (as well as plans to improve facilities for temporary aircraft berthing there).[80] But the Navy can go well beyond the idea of stationing three submarines there; in fact, there is room to add at least eight more, according to the Congressional Budget Office. There are huge efficiencies to be gained by doing so. The average number of mission days for a submarine stationed so near the Western Pacific theater might be about 100 a year, roughly three times what a submarine stationed in the continental United States can muster. The benefits of homeporting more attack submarines on Guam would be twofold: one, it would ensure faster response during a crisis, and, two, it would make the submarine fleet more efficient. This latter fact might allow cost savings through a downsizing of the attack submarine force. To give a specific example, adding six more submarines to Guam would allow a reduction of ten to twelve attack submarines in the force structure and would save an annual average of more than $1 billion without a reduction in mission effectiveness.[81] Better yet, the force structure could be reduced by eight submarines—yielding some budgetary savings as well as some net increase in overall military capability.

Forward-homeporting need not be limited to the attack submarine fleet. Even with the Navy's fleet response program, homeporting a second carrier closer to a key theater of operations makes good sense. The idea of moving a carrier from California to either Hawaii or Guam merits serious attention.[82] By previous patterns of carrier deployments, homeports in California necessitated travels of some two weeks to East Asia and three or more weeks to the Persian Gulf.[83] Homeporting in Hawaii or Guam can shave five to ten days off that time, each way.

A carrier based further west in the Pacific may prove somewhat more vulnerable tactically than one based back home—good reason not to extend this idea to several carriers. But on the other side of things, stationing multiple carriers in a single port *anywhere* creates the possibility of a single point of failure or vulnerability. So taking an aircraft carrier out of a port like San Diego where several are normally present and instead stationing it in Hawaii or Guam where we presently have none makes logical sense from a force protection standpoint as well. Although it seems unlikely to be possible given political constraints in Japan, there is even an argument for homeporting a second carrier there, whether in Yokosuka or somewhere else.[84]

Making the transition could be expensive; indeed, simply moving 8,000 marines and their dependents to Guam and providing for training and other logistical support for them is now estimated to cost $15 billion. But with aircraft carriers, forward-homeporting can lead to a smaller carrier fleet. If it were to cost say $5 billion to $7 billion for permanent basing of a carrier on Guam, that would roughly equal the costs of building just one carrier itself—not to mention its aircraft and surface escorts. Since having a carrier forward-stationed can provide as much forward presence as three to five based in the United States, a plan that put a carrier on Guam, while reducing one in the overall force structure, would therefore save money while increasing forward presence capabilities.[85] Annual savings would average out to about $2 billion a year.[86]

EUROPE

The downsizing of U.S. forces in Europe in general, and of Army forces in Germany in particular, is sound. But it should be noted that German bases have virtues. The quality of life for U.S. forces in Germany has been good; the access to port facilities in times of crisis or war has been excellent, even when governments in the United States and Germany disagreed about the wisdom of carrying out a given military operation; the costs to the United States of having substantial troops in Europe, above and beyond what those costs would be for troops in the United States, are real but moderate.[87] Even so, these arguments are balanced by reasons to downsize and relocate, consolidating more U.S. troops at home.

That said, the Rumsfeld plans went too far. It appears that Secretary Gates agrees with that assessment, but it is worth laying out the argument in any event, since some of the debates may resume, particularly if and when current wars end and some consider the idea of again modestly downsizing the nation's ground forces. The first reason that Rumsfeld's plan for U.S. forces in Europe overreached concerns the matter of operational tempo. Some of the changes proposed for the U.S. Army could worsen an overdeployment problem that is presently posing the greatest challenge to the all-volunteer force in its thirty-five-year history. Given the ongoing strains of the Iraq and Afghanistan missions, it simply does not make sense to take large numbers of Army soldiers out of bases in Germany, where they can be accompanied by their families, and deploy soldiers on unescorted tours to eastern Europe. At least as of fairly recently, Pentagon plans appeared to envision stationing a brigade of forces at a time in Romania or Bulgaria or both countries; this seems a bad idea for the foreseeable future given the strains on the force. Whether more soldiers are kept in Germany or stationed in the United States, they should not be deployed to eastern Europe in large numbers while the Iraq and Afghanistan wars continue to take soldiers away from their home bases and families so much already.

Removing all four heavy brigades from Germany may be too much for another reason as well: it would reduce the opportunities for joint training and exercises with European heavy forces. This concern has also been expressed by retired general Montgomery Meigs, former head of U.S. Army forces in Europe.[88] Leaving at least one existing heavy brigade in Europe, as well as the 173rd airborne brigade, while introducing a Stryker brigade, may make for a better mix and a more adequate overall set of capabilities.[89] At a minimum, this possibility should be examined.[90] While Germany itself is hardly at risk from a threat that would require tank-heavy units to counterattack, NATO remains the United States' paramount institution for responding militarily to threats around the world—and Germany remains the main place where U.S. Army units train with their NATO counterparts (even if such combined training occurs less frequently than might be ideal). Depriving European Command of all traditional armored and mechanized infantry units would risk weakening broader alliance preparations for heavy combat, be it in the Persian Gulf or East Asia or elsewhere.[91]

AFRICOM

The concept of Africa Command, operational as of October 1, 2008, has had a somewhat troubled start. That is unfortunate, because the motivation for devoting a regional command to the African continent is quite reasonable and reflected a sensitivity by DoD to the appropriateness of such an organization. Until the creation of AFRICOM, Africa was addressed by European Command (if at all) and as such rarely received serious attention from the U.S. armed forces.

One or more training facilities should be considered, perhaps under African Union auspices, that could host forces from several countries at once. The United States might team with certain other major powers and allies in helping create such facilities. To improve interoperability with U.S. forces, and each other, African militaries would be well served by such facilities that brought numbers of units from different places together all at once. In addition, these facilities would constitute important symbolic and rhetorical confirmation of the United States' commitment to the continent. According to the estimated need of missions or potential missions from Darfur to the Congo to Somalia and elsewhere, the African continent could usefully expand its peace operations capacity by as much as 50,000 or more troops, above and beyond those that have been helped to date by U.S. training and equipping programs, as argued above as well.[92]

But the military role of the United States in Africa is not just a matter of increasing capacity, however appropriate that may be. It also requires attention to projecting the right image to the continent and ensuring that the U.S. role there is not overmilitarized. This concern has emerged in the context of Africa Command, which is beginning its existence in the very non-African country of Germany. African friends have been reluctant to go along with the political and strategic baggage of hosting the command on their soil. This is understandable, and for many of them, the strategically correct decision.[93] However, if and when a solidly democratic African partner state decides that it would like to host AFRICOM's headquarters, the United States should take that idea very seriously. It is true that U.S. military commands devoted to other regions of the world often have their headquarters on U.S. territory (this is true for Central Command, Southern Command, and Pacific Command); in fact, European Command is the only such organization truly based within its relevant area of responsibility. So Africa is not being treated differently from most parts of the world. That said, the logic of regional commands should generally argue for situating headquarters as close to the area of responsibility as possible.

Going beyond the simple question of location, if AFRICOM's image and effectiveness are to change, the soft power dimensions of U.S. foreign policy must improve to create the perception and reality of a more balanced approach. General Kip Ward, head of AFRICCOM, is already voicing a strong message of interagency cooperation and support for the real needs of African nations, but more needs to be done.[94] Increases in foreign assistance certainly have a role. Another worthy idea, advanced by Ambassador Robert Oakley and Michael Casey, is to take steps to make clear that a U.S. ambassador in a given country is the senior U.S. official there and that he or she is in charge of all U.S. assets, including military ones, in the country in question. That may require allowing the ambassador, working with interagency country teams, to have more say over U.S. resource allocation within a given country. Also, the ambassador always should be apprised of the presence and the activities of U.S. military personnel in his country of responsibility and should generally share that information with the host nation. There is apparent movement in this direction and it should continue.[95]

CHAPTER FIVE

HOMELAND SECURITY

MORE THAN SEVEN YEARS after the attacks of September 11, 2001, where does the United States stand in trying to ensure that such a terrible tragedy—or something even worse—never again befalls this country?

Answering this question requires attention to a broad gamut of policy tools, many of them in the provinces of foreign, defense, and intelligence policy. The United States cannot, in the end, be secure if its allies and partners around the world are not and if international terrorism flourishes even in distant lands. Such was part of the lesson of 9/11, with those attacks originating in Afghanistan, Saudi Arabia, and other parts of the broader Middle East. Many subsequent terrorist attacks around the world have come from equally remote territory in Pakistan's frontier provinces, in the tribal belts of Yemen, and elsewhere. But part of the answer to the question also relates to the somewhat more circumscribed policy area of homeland security—defined here as defending the homeland against "national hazards, whether they are man made or nature made, across the entire spectrum of prevention, protection, and response." This broad yet crisp definition was provided by the then secretary of homeland security Michael Chertoff at Brookings in September 2008.[1]

Homeland security itself involves international cooperation; it is not to be mistaken with creation of a fortress America. Foreign partners are needed to verify what goods are on ships and airplanes, to check passenger names on aircraft manifests, and the like. But for analytical specificity, it is defined here somewhat restrictively as impeding the actions of those already committed to this nation's harm as they seek to enter the United States or operate within it.

Homeland security has improved considerably over the last seven years, but there are still many gaps that demand attention. Although some economies in existing programs may be possible, the emphasis here is on identifying remaining national gaps in preparedness. That is because the United States still has some acute vulnerabilities and shortfalls of preparation in what remains a relatively new type of federal effort (and a very young new federal department). That said, some do call for massive new homeland defense programs, and I take a somewhat skeptical eye to these, as discussed further below.

THE BASIC BUDGET PICTURE

Aggregate spending on homeland security has of course increased greatly in modern times. It totaled roughly $4 billion to $6 billion annually in the 1980s, rose modestly to about $7 billion annually in the first Bush administration, and grew substantially to $15 billion a year by the end of the Clinton administration. It is now about $40 billion a year, having nearly tripled over the course of the George W. Bush presidency in response to 9/11.

There are different ways to track spending now. One way is in funding for the actual Department of Homeland Security. The Obama administration's request for 2010 of $42.7 billion in discretionary funding is an increase relative to the $40.1 billion level for 2009 (although 2009 also had one-time homeland security funds of about $2.2 billion for the Bioshield program and $2.8 billion in Recovery Act money that are not included in that $40.1 billion figure).[2]

These figures for DHS budgets are not the same as actual homeland security budgets. DHS accounts include some functions not directly tied to homeland security (such as many Coast Guard activities for boater safety and the like). They also exclude relevant activities by the Departments of Defense, Health and Human Services (HHS), Justice, State, and others. Once adjustments are made, actually homeland security budgets have followed a similar trajectory to that indicated above.[3] The Bush administration request for homeland security for 2009 actually totaled some $66 billion, though this figure overstates actual costs to the taxpayer because a number of user fees and other sources of revenue mitigate the need for direct federal appropriations. Broken down by agency, to use analyst Steven Kosiak's phrase, most funds go to the "big six": DHS, $32.8 billion (this figure does not count DHS's activities outside of direct security functions, which are numerous); Defense, $17.6 billion; HHS, $4.5 billion; Justice, $3.8 billion; State, $2.5 billion; and Energy, $1.9 billion (see table 5-1).[4]

Homeland security funding can also be subdivided by function. The 2009 Bush budget request allocated $25.7 billion for border and transportation security (mostly for the Department of Homeland Security), $20.1 billion for protecting critical infrastructure (mostly for DoD, to protect bases), $9.1 billion for defending against catastrophic threats (the majority to DoD, another large chunk to HHS), $5.4 billion for domestic counterterrorism (the majority to the Department of Justice for FBI activities), $5.0 billion for emergency preparedness and response (the largest chunks to HHS and DHS), and just under $1.0 billion for other costs, mostly intelligence and warning (most to DHS and Justice).

Within DHS, the main subagencies and spending categories are as follows, again in reference to the 2009 budget request. Customs and Border Protection was to receive $9.5 billion; Immigration and Customs Enforcement, $4.7 billion; the Transportation Security Administration, $4.1 billion; the U.S. Coast Guard, $9.1 billion; the U.S. Secret Service, $1.4 billion; the Federal Emergency Management Administration (FEMA), $5.6 billion (including $2.2 billion in grants to states and localities); and the Domestic Nuclear Detection Office about $0.6 billion.[5]

THE STATE OF HOMELAND SECURITY

The threat of terrorism remains significant, and hence the rationale for focusing on homeland security remains quite strong. Global terror trends have leveled off but remain at a high level, with upward of 4,000 serious attacks a year (that is, those resulting in at least one death, injury, or kidnapping) through mid-decade, not even counting Iraq and Afghanistan.[6] Truck bombings and suicide attacks have also continued, from Algeria and Yemen to Iraq and Afghanistan to Pakistan and India,

TABLE 5-1. Federal Homeland Security Funding by Agency, FY 2002–09 [a]

Budget authority in millions of dollars

Department	FY 2002	FY 2003	FY 2004	FY 2005	FY 2006	FY 2007	FY 2008	FY 2009	FY 2009 as percentage of total
Department of Homeland Security (DHS)	17,381	23,063	22,923	24,549	26,571	29,554	32,740	32,817	49.5
Department of Defense (DOD) [b]	16,126	8,442	7,024	17,188	17,510	16,538	17,374	17,646	26.6
Department of Health and Human Services (HHS)	1,913	4,144	4,062	4,229	4,352	4,327	4,301	4,457	6.7
Department of Justice (DOJ)	2,143	2,349	2,180	2,767	3,026	3,518	3,523	3,795	5.7
Department of State (DOS)	477	634	696	824	1,108	1,242	1,962	2,466	3.7
Department of Energy (DOE)	1,220	1,408	1,364	1,562	1,702	1,719	1,829	1,943	2.9
Department of Agriculture (AG)	553	410	411	596	597	541	570	691	1.0
National Science Foundation (NSF)	260	285	340	342	344	385	374	379	0.6
Department of Veterans Affairs (VA)	49	154	271	249	298	260	272	348	0.5
Department of Commerce	116	112	125	167	181	205	207	262	0.4
Other agencies	3,613	1,445	1,437	1,910	1,429	1,545	1,772	1,500	2.3
Total federal budget authority	43,848	42,447	40,834	54,383	57,118	59,833	64,923	66,303	100

Source: Congressional Research Service, "Homeland Security Department: FY2009 Appropriations," CRS Report for Congress RL34482 (Washington, up-dated March 4, 2009), p. 112 (www.fas.org/sgp/crs/homesec/RL34482.pdf).

a. Totals may not add due to rounding. Fiscal year (FY) totals shown in this table include enacted supplemental funding. Year-to-year comparisons may not be directly comparable, because as time has gone on agencies have been able to distinguish homeland security and non-homeland security activities with greater specificity. Totals include discretionary and mandatory funds.

b. FY 2002, FY 2003, and FY 2004 do not include reestimates of DoD homeland security funding. For FY 2007 DOD changed the manner in which it calculates its homeland security activities. This new method of estimation has been applied for FY 2005 and forward. Reestimates of FY 2002 to FY 2004 DOD funding using this new method of calculation were not available for inclusion.

with the horrific late November 2008 attacks in Mumbai a vivid reminder of the ongoing problem. Ominously, a plot hatched largely in Pakistan to bomb some ten airplanes in flight as they crossed the Atlantic from Britain to the United States was uncovered in 2006. Thankfully it was thwarted, but the sophistication of the plan was considerable. The idea was to bring explosives aboard in beverage containers that had been drained of their original contents through small holes in the bottom of the containers and then, after the explosive components were introduced, resealed carefully in a way that made the containers appear unopened. The contents would then be linked to simple detonators constructed out of normal batteries and detonated in flight.[7] Because of such activities and such plots, analysts such as Bruce Riedel and Bruce Hoffman convincingly argue that al Qaeda and related organizations remain quite dangerous.[8]

While the threat remains serious, homeland security is much improved since 9/11. Starting with the most obvious issue area, airplanes are much more difficult to hijack. Passenger manifests are now being more carefully checked against terrorist watch lists, cockpit doors are hardened, and pilots as well as passengers are far less inclined to tolerate any threatening acts by would-be hijackers.[9]

Intelligence stovepipes have been broken down, so that different federal intelligence agencies share information and warnings more routinely, with each other and to some extent with state and local officials as well. A culture of guarding information very closely according to a "need to know" paradigm has been largely replaced with a philosophy of "responsibility to provide" information among intelligence agencies.[10] Terrorist watch lists have been better integrated, both domestically and internationally, through the highly regarded work of the National Counterterrorism Center and other agencies of government.[11]

Joint Terrorism Task Forces have been established by the FBI in 100 of the country's major cities and now employ nearly 4,000 people, most of them FBI special agents. Some forty state or regional fusion centers, each staffed by twenty-five to thirty persons, have been created to integrate and share information with the federal government and within their states on terrorism-related activities, persons, and issues. They are often a crime fighting tool as well; for example, in Chicago they are informed by hundreds of video cameras and gunfire detection systems watching certain dangerous parts of the city.[12] They are funded largely by the states and localities, although the federal government has contributed several hundred million dollars too (and should continue to do so).[13] There are still too many disparate data systems and classification systems and too many unclear channels of communication in these various ventures and these agencies. But the progress has been considerable nonetheless.[14]

Procedures are in place with the Department of Homeland Security, the Department of Defense's Northern Command (NORTHCOM), the nation's governors, the National Guard, and other key players to expedite communications in a crisis. Fiascos such as what happened recently with Hurricane Katrina in 2005 are now less likely. Most governments at all levels across the United States have now complied with requirements under the National Incident Management System to create communications channels and basic coordination plans for responding to catastrophes.[15] This reflects important progress.[16]

Passport and visa documents are much more dependable, harder to forge or fake or otherwise misuse. For example, the United States is now gradually moving to take ten fingerprints rather than just two of those entering the country and to improve its ability to match potential terrorists to fingerprints taken at crime scenes and other such places around the world. As of 2007, all new passports issued by the United States are e-passports, containing a chip that can store a digital photograph of the passport holder and other key information (and with numerous types of shielding and encryption employed to thwart illicit probing of the data on the passports by individuals without a right to that information). Those countries operating within the visa waiver program (or VWP, meaning that their citizens need not obtain visas for travel to the United States) are issuing e-passports as well. They are to use an improved form of identification such as fingerprints by 2009 (although older American and VWP passports remain in use, without such features).[17]

Concerns about hostile individuals with passports from participating VWP countries have led the United States to create other instruments for monitoring travel by various individuals. These include not only data exchanges on airline passengers, but also now an Electronic System for Travel Authorization (ESTA) that is mandated for individuals from VWP countries before travel to the United States.[18] Thus the United States is trying to close any loopholes that result from the visa waiver program system. Biometric indicators are being widely deployed in the above types of efforts. They are helping to keep about 5,000 suspicious people a year out of the United States (as of 2006).[19]

In addition to greater cooperation on issues such as sharing data and improving the security of identification and passports, many foreign countries have also stepped up their counterterrorism capacities substantially in areas such as intelligence.[20]

Prominent buildings and other public gathering spots are now partially protected in the United States. For example, by 2006, for 58 percent of all high-priority critical infrastructure in the United States, a buffer-zone protection plan had been implemented to control access to relevant assets.[21] Toxic chemical plants must now file plant security plans with the federal government, which scrutinizes the plans and sometimes demands better preparations and stronger measures, with the possibility of levying fines against noncompliant firms.[22]

Significant progress has been made toward procuring antidotes against certain biological agents, like anthrax or smallpox, with millions of doses of antidotes now stockpiled. In fact, 300 million doses of smallpox vaccine have been procured, enough for the whole population.[23] Significant steps have also been taken to prepare some parts of the nation's military as well as its first responder community to handle chemical attacks and other such threats, as noted elsewhere in more detail.

A few additional statistics are illuminating. As of 2003, no part of the U.S. open border was truly controlled; by fiscal year 2007, about 600 miles were at least partially controlled (even though fences were often breached or otherwise circumvented).[24] Over the same period, the fraction of container cargo headed for U.S. ports that was processed overseas (not necessarily inspected, but monitored in some way) rose from 0 to 86 percent, the fraction of containers arriving in U.S. ports that was scanned with sophisticated remote technology went from 0 to 4 percent, and the fraction of containers arriving by truck or rail that was scanned went from 0 to 40 percent. Whether thoroughly inspected or not, the fraction of cargo that went through radiation detection grew from 0 to 94 percent by 2007. The number of bioaerosol collectors deployed in top threat cities increased from 206 at the end of 2003 to 527 by the end of 2007. Of DHS's thirty-five quick response teams for helping communities affected by disaster or terrorism, none were deemed ready in 2003 but almost all met requisite criteria by 2007. No government agencies could document solid plans for maintaining continuity of essential operations after a catastrophic disaster in 2003; 80 percent could do so by the end of 2007.[25]

However, for all the progress, the list of enduring vulnerabilities is almost as long. The flip side of many of these statistics is that most goals are not yet met—and in some cases, those goals are themselves not sufficiently ambitious in the first place.

Internationally, while terror watch lists have become much better integrated, and terrorist-financing blacklists have become more rigorously enforced to police the illicit flow of funds for dangerous organizations, backsliding is possible. For example, there are now legal challenges to some of the financing blacklists within the European justice system.[26]

The Border Patrol has been increased in size from 9,000 to 20,000, but most land borders are still fairly easy to penetrate. Progress is being made toward screening cargo carried on passenger airlines, and 100 percent screening is expected by 2010, but most cargo reaching the country by sea still is not thoroughly examined (as noted above). The screening that is taking place for such cargo may not be an adequate substitute for actual inspection and will require constant monitoring and improvement.

Standards for reliable identification remain too weak in some states; some driver's licenses should make better use of biometric indicators and digitization technologies for verifying proper ownership. The Real ID Act will require states to do so soon, for those wishing to use their driver's licenses as proof of identity to travel on airplanes or enter federal buildings.[27] But not all states may comply fully.

Trains and subways remain inherently soft and unprotected targets in general. Only about half of key transportation assets or systems have developed risk mitigation strategies. Moreover, this figure applies only to planning and not actual implementation.[28] More broadly, only very few cities devote substantial police resources to address terrorism threats.

Hospitals are not ready to treat victims of chemical or biological attack for the most part. While more antidote has been procured for some specific biological threats, methods for developing, producing, stockpiling, and above all distributing vaccines against biological agents are wanting to date. The nation's food supply is not particularly well secured. Better biological weapons detectors are being developed, but they would usually pick up an agent only four hours after dispersal—an improvement relative to current methods but still far short of the ideal.[29]

The country's military still has limited capacity for rapid response for domestic emergencies. NORTHCOM does have about 8,000 troops on call to help with emergencies, but they may not have the attributes needed to respond effectively. Procedures for helping the National Guard organize regionally, so that neighboring states may help each other more dependably and quickly in major crises, are still informal and fairly weak. National Guard links with NORTHCOM appear better, and more equipment may have been predeployed to states where it is most likely to be needed, but the ability of Guard units to help each other promptly and directly is less developed.[30]

The Homeland Security Council (HSC) in the White House remains insufficiently integrated with other key agencies, most notably the National Security Council (NSC). At this point, HSC should probably be merged with the NSC, not least because many of HSC's efforts involve partnering with other countries and as such require proper coordination with those arms of government that typically cooperate across international lines.[31]

About half of the nation's main stadiums and other large public arenas are partially protected against terrorism, the other half are not. Trucks carrying hazardous materials are not amply protected at all stages in their normal operations. Except perhaps in New York, large buildings are generally not being better outfitted with simple counterterror capabilities, even when being refit or built anew—shatterproof glass in lobbies is not used enough, air intakes are still too easily accessible.

Some hypothetical threats remain sufficiently low in probability, or sufficiently hard to address, that they may not merit immediate major remedial action. But they should be kept in mind nonetheless. Airliners are not protected against surface-to-air missiles. The nation's coasts and borders are not protected against cruise missiles. Moreover, Hamas-style terrorism (of a smaller scale than what al Qaeda prefers) could still pose a mid-level threat to the nation's malls, movie theaters, and other moderate-sized buildings (as with the November 2008 attacks in Mumbai, India). No Israel-style defenses such as metal detectors at entrances to public facilities have been developed for such places.

As noted, not all hypothetical vulnerabilities must be addressed. Trying to do so could bankrupt the country. In addition, as Brookings scholar Jeremy Shapiro has argued, al Qaeda and affiliates seem to have a strong proclivity for certain types of attacks—principally those involving airplanes and truck bombs—as well as a penchant to attempt only the spectacular against U.S.-based targets. Having overachieved, so to speak, on 9/11, they are reluctant to attempt garden-variety terrorism. They might believe that such smaller attacks would fail to live up to the standards and expectations they have created among their followers as well as the American and global publics. Moreover, while they may still harbor some hopes of being able to attack with weapons of mass destruction, their capacity to do so given the state of the global al Qaeda diaspora and network is extremely limited. On balance, as Shapiro argues fairly convincingly, they are probably not inclined to attack economic targets such as ports, food distribution systems, and information systems, moderately unlikely to employ Hamas-style low-level attacks, and quite unlikely to have access to weapons of mass destruction (especially the most threatening types).[32]

Even for one taking a somewhat less sanguine view than Shapiro, practical considerations have to compete with worst-case planning. Many targets are extremely hard to protect, meaning that the premium should be on stronger prevention (through intelligence and border controls and the like) rather than on site defense or consequence management. And some types of attacks are worse than others, suggesting that the country should indeed focus primary attention on catastrophic risks rather than on more modest ones. This is one reason, among others, why the Department of Homeland Security needs stronger analytical capacity to evaluate threats and possible responses to those threats—a better planning process, akin to what the Department of Defense has developed over the years in units such as the Office of Program Analysis and Evaluation and Office of Net Assessment.[33] Existing procedures focused on fifteen national planning scenarios have been used either within the military, at NORTHCOM, or in a somewhat weak interagency form through the Incident Management Planning Team. Some have suggested that this process instead be handled through the National Security Council, but the NSC is typically not an excellent place to do planning given its limited size and capacities. DHS seems the more natural and appropriate place, even for interagency work that includes other federal agencies as well as state and local actors. The Office of Management and Budget (OMB) should also be involved in these planning efforts; budgetary discipline is as noted a critical part of any homeland security planning process.[34] But the main point is that DHS needs a much stronger capacity in this area.

This framework for identifying homeland security priorities—focus on preventive efforts, on catastrophic threats, on the types of attacks already preferred (or actively contemplated and planned) by al Qaeda, and also, where possible, on activities that provide additional benefits beyond the security sphere—was introduced in earlier Brookings Institution work. It guides my analysis below as well. It also argues against some recent proposals for America's homeland security efforts, such as books entitled *America the Vulnerable* and *Open Target,* which take a more sweeping view of where the country's vulnerabilities remain and favor a greater allocation of resources to address them.

To be sure, many of the concrete ideas offered in the above books are worthwhile.[35] But some ideas heard in the debate are less sound. One report recommended spending $20 billion a year equipping all of the nation's first responders with chemical and biological protective gear, as well as interoperable communications systems. In a similar spirit, some have advocated viewing the National Guard as primarily a homeland defense and security organization, requiring the active military as well as the Reserves to handle all overseas missions—implying the likely need to increase the ranks of these latter two by several hundred thousand personnel. Others advocate 100 percent monitoring of cargo shipping or a completely secure land border or defenses against surface-to-air missiles (SAMs) for all domestic airliners. Ideas for a national cruise missile defense, for hospital wards in every city devoted to the victims of possible biological weapons attack, and for mandatory and comprehensive security standards for many of the nation's chemical plants have also been discussed.

Future events could change the calculus on some of these. If a plane is shot down by a SAM, passengers will likely insist on countermeasures before flying again. If a chemical plant is successfully attacked, a security plan that relies principally on industry cooperation, as is the case today, may seem insufficient. If a contagious biological attack occurs in the future, the kind of scare that occurred during the anthrax attacks of 2001—only much worse, given the potential for human-to-human transmission—it could provoke further action.

However, a comprehensive approach to homeland security gaps could very easily cost the nation $50 billion a year more, on top of roughly that amount already being spent by the federal government on homeland security today. Given the scarcity of resources, and the need to address more fundamental causes of terrorism abroad, that would seem a questionable use of resources. My suggestions are guided by a more economical philosophy. The following initiatives seem worthy of additional resource expenditure or, at a minimum, serious and detailed examination, but in each case, I attempt to find an approach that makes sense on cost-benefit grounds.

AIRPLANES

For all the improvements in air safety, al Qaeda retains a fixation on using or destroying airplanes and a continued tendency to look for weaknesses in our defenses. And those weaknesses still exist. Weapons can still be snuck through checkpoints, for example, as various auditors and investigators have proven in recent years. So can explosives. These concerns place a premium on improving the quality of sensors used to look for explosives and sharp objects on individuals.[36]

As of early 2009, 50 percent of all cargo carried in the bays of passenger jets is to be screened. It should be noted that screening is a modest, perhaps insufficient standard for security—it does *not* equate to physically inspecting all cargo (or hardening cargo bays against possible bombs in cargo), which some have suggested as the more appropriate goal. At a minimum, then, it will be important to meet the objective of 100 percent screening by August 2010. In addition, since screening is to be done largely by companies vouching for their own goods and products, an effective certification process will have to be established to ensure that private firms are doing the job adequately. The 9/11 Commission Act of 2007 is ambiguous about whether inbound cargo from abroad must also be screened. The simple, obvious answer is that yes it should be.[37] The added cost of all these improved explosive detection systems and other modifications may be $150 million a year or so above the 2009 budget request of $122 million.[38]

Certain steps to improve aviation security that one might assume to have already been done have not, in fact, all been completed as of this writing. For example, it took until October 2008 for the Transportation Security Administration to propose a rule that large private aircraft (of 12,500 pounds maximum takeoff weight or more) must have crews and passengers checked against terrorism watch lists.[39] Given their potential to be used as guided missiles, even smaller planes should probably be so certified.

Air marshals now number in the thousands, permitting perhaps 10 percent of the 28,000 daily flights in the United States to have them aboard. Hardened cockpit doors may suffice as a counterhijacking method, but the adequacy of this number of marshals can be questioned. Admittedly, the "brute force" approach of having marshals aboard all flights may not be worth the cost. Increasing the air marshal force by a factor of ten could cost $2 billion a year. But it has to be something of an open question whether the current capacity is adequate. After all, the fact that air marshals are considered necessary on any flight makes one wonder why they are not deployed on virtually all flights.[40] It is doubtful that our intelligence is really so exquisite as to know which flights *might* have unknown and unidentified terrorists aboard. More likely, we are deploying air marshals on the flights that we consider most likely to be hijacked given the size of aircraft and the cities between which they are traveling. But since almost any domestic flight will have enough fuel aboard to be within range of some large city, the logic of a minimalist approach to using air marshals may not be airtight. Without access to all the classified information necessary to do a thorough cost-benefit assessment, my instinct is to believe that the air marshal program should expand by as much as 50 to 100 percent—meaning up to $200 million annually.

What about the surface-to-air missile threat? This is a serious concern, as the attempted downing of a commercial jet in Kenya in 2002 reminded us all. SAMs have brought down jumbo jets before, and there are many of them still feared to be loose around the world. They are also not easy to find if hidden within a shipping container, or for that matter a sailboat crossing the Great Lakes or a vehicle transiting the U.S.-Mexican border. In principle we know what to do about SAMs—put infrared countermeasures on airplanes, perhaps also deploy countermeasure systems at airports, and if absolutely necessary, employ airports that are far enough away from urban centers that airport perimeters can be well patrolled and nearby areas also monitored. In practice, these steps would cost tens of billions of dollars to implement. So the practical near-term approach is probably to keep perfecting countermeasure technology and keep planning for how to keep air traffic going in the days and weeks after any successful (or even unsuccessful, but worrisome) attack—yet not to deploy the expensive, imperfect systems until the threat crystallizes or the relevant technology is further improved.[41]

Border Patrol

The Border Patrol has been increased in size from 9,000 to 20,000, but most land borders are still fairly easy to penetrate. The United States government has not, at least as of early 2008 according to a statement of NORTHCOM commander General Victor Renuart, yet witnessed any attempt by terrorists to cross over the Mexican border to gain access to the country. But that could clearly change.[42] The goal of homeland security policy should not be the absolute (and unrealistic) fortification of the nation's borders, but rather a gradual and ongoing expansion of fencing, sensing, and agents for response. This is an issue where one has to feel out the situation as one expands gradually. Since the metric of perfect protection is unattainable, the goal will always be to use existing resources as efficiently as possible to complicate, deter, or (if necessary, and if lucky) interdict the attempted entry of a terrorist into the country via a land border. Right now, the border is still far too porous, as proven by the continued large, illicit flows of people into the country, so the steady buildup in capacity should continue.[43]

Efforts to deploy a Secure Border Initiative, including up to 670 miles of fencing and an associated network of sensors for monitoring movements in the most heavily trafficked areas of the southern border, have been slow to move forward. As of late 2008, only about half the planned fencing had been deployed, and the SBI*net* sensor system was about three years behind schedule, with likely completion not before 2011.[44] Some delays are understandable, but it makes sense to do what is possible to accelerate and properly fund this effort. Considering delays in this program, and the still-thin ranks of Border Police, at least another $250 million a year is warranted for the land borders. The Obama budget proposal appears to agree.[45]

In addition, it is incumbent upon the United States to ensure humane treatment for any and all detainees that result from border enforcement actions. At present that does not occur; medical and legal help can be lacking, and budgets for taking care of detainees have not kept up with the increased caseloads since 9/11. An additional $50 million a year is justified to address these concerns—and to ensure that there is not a backlash, at home or abroad, against efforts to tighten borders.[46]

SEA BORDERS AND THE COAST GUARD

The United States has enormous littoral borders—95,000 miles of coastline.[47] These include many ports that are particularly vulnerable to maritime attacks. Although workers at the ports are increasingly subject to security checks, with full compliance mandated by mid-2009, other threats remain. These include the possibility of small boats or even robotic semi-submersibles being used in attacks against larger ships, akin to the *Cole* attack in Yemen in 2000. Large ships are being brought into a program called the Automatic Identification System and tracked when in or near ports, but smaller vessels are not to be part of the network.[48] Perhaps it is not realistic to include them. However, if that is the case, other measures such as clearly marked keep-out zones might have to be employed more thoroughly in ports where ships with toxic, flammable, or otherwise highly dangerous cargo could be attacked.[49]

Today's Coast Guard has grown and received more resources since 9/11. Its annual real budget was below $6 billion in 2000–01 (in 2009 dollars) and now exceeds $9 billion. Its total manpower has grown but by less than 20 percent since that time, relative to a cold war norm that was fairly steady from the 1960s onward.[50] To wit, its current active duty end strength is about 42,000, in contrast to averages of 35,000 historically. This may not be enough, however. The Coast Guard also may have inadequate resources even to keep its current force structure in good operational shape. As of 2006, for example, only 62 percent of its key assets met readiness standards of good or excellent, a decline from previous years.[51]

The most logical way to think of properly funding the Coast Guard is to ensure that three conditions are met:

—Ongoing readiness and modernization agendas should be properly funded.

—The added demands of homeland security should not further weaken other types of Coast Guard missions, such as boater safety and environmental monitoring, that were already underfunded before 9/11, as well as cooperation with Mexico and other partners in monitoring waters used by drug traffickers (and potentially a greater Coast Guard role in overseas coalition operations such as counterpiracy missions near Somalia).

—Some added emphasis on new security missions, such as greater harbor security as noted above, should be feasible.

The first objective seems on the way to being met. While readiness figures for the Coast Guard remain mediocre, modernization programs are finally in acceptable shape and should improve that readiness steadily without large quantities of additional resources. However, while the Coast Guard has grown by 15 percent since 9/11, homeland security activities account for 25 to 40 percent of its total missions—meaning that other types of activities have often been cut back.[52] This simple metric suggests a further 10 percent growth in the fleet—half to ensure that nonsecurity missions not be shortchanged, the other to allow for better port and harbor protection. That in turn would require budgetary growth of perhaps $900 million in the annual budget.

MASS TRANSIT

Protecting trains, light rail, subways, and buses is even harder than ensuring airline security. More than twice as many people take the New York subway every day as take airplanes nationwide, for example, and subway passengers are generally in even more of a hurry than plane passengers and use many more entrance and egress points.[53]

Particularly for light rail, subways, and buses—decentralized systems carrying lots of passengers, usually on short trips—complete screening of all passengers and luggage is almost out of the question. While theoretically possible, it would be hugely disruptive, very expensive, and not attainable within a short time frame even if determined to be a necessary goal.

What to do in this situation? Alas, incrementalism and opportunism must be the watchwords, along with constant feedback to maximize the use of scarce resources like officers and canine teams. Certain other steps can be considered too. For example, random checks of baggage and passengers on subways can be increased, as has been done in New York and now in Washington, D.C.[54] More random inspections should probably occur on Amtrak as well; they are currently quite infrequent.[55]

New York City has been building a monitoring system with 1,000 surveillance cameras and 3,000 motion sensors for its subway and light rail systems. Delays have arisen, and costs have grown upward to $500 million, but the concept is generally sound for New York, given the threat. It might be needed in some other cities (crime fighting considerations also argue for it).[56] As Richard Clarke points out, establishing regulations on how such surveillance technology is used, and involving outside voices like the ACLU to help in placing constraints on use, is the most effective way to reassure those concerned about their liberties being impinged upon.[57] More use of police and canine teams also makes sense (and could be provided by some of the added police officers that the federal government would help fund under the idea presented below).

LOCAL POLICE COUNTERTERRORISM CAPACITY

With the exception of New York City; Washington, D.C.; Los Angeles; and one or two other main urban areas, cities do not take the terrorism threat very seriously and do not devote many key police resources to address it. New York has perhaps 500 to 700 police dedicated to counterterrorism and again as many involved in counterterrorism-related activities (such as subway monitoring) on a given day; even in proportionate terms, most other cities are dramatically below this level of effort.

Some ideas for dramatically expanding local capacities against terrorism seem unwarranted, especially if their expense competes with programs addressing more imminent threats to most U.S. urban populations such as violent crime. However, modest and practical steps still make sense. As suggested by L.A. councilman Jack Weiss, for example, local police and first responder groups should have mobile vans for interoperable communications. They should also have small, dedicated units capable of handling toxic, radioactive, or other such threats (and helping local hospitals determine how to handle any resulting casualties). Nationwide, the costs for such programs might total in the general range of $500 million a year and as such should already be affordable with existing grant programs if funds are used well.[58] Some jurisdictions such as the greater Chicago area and the state of Illinois, for example, are already acquiring such capabilities.[59]

In addition, more police departments of large urban areas need to create dedicated counterterrorism units—if not on the scale of New York City's (even once adjusted for population), then still typically into the dozens of individuals. In some cases, given how local police precincts operate, this will require either merging numerous small law enforcement agencies into larger metropolitan forces—or at least, pooling resources to create capacity at the regional level. The increased capacity of Joint Terrorism Task Forces as well as fusion centers has helped. Further progress can occur with greater standardization of suspicious activity reports (SARs) and other intelligence tools designed to organize and share information.[60]

Washington might try to boost this process further by creating a "Community Oriented Policing Services (COPS) II" program—modeled after the Clinton administration's crime fighting initiative of the 1990s (though on a much smaller scale in this case). For example, the federal government might offer to pay half the salary of up to twenty counterterrorism officers for every million people in a given metropolitan area, for cities of a certain size. Applied nationally, it might lead to the hiring of 1,000 additional police officers, with the federal share of the yearly tab a modest $100 million. The goal should be to have more cities do, proportionately, what Los Angeles has done: increasing its capacity from some thirty counterterrorism officers a few years ago to more than 100 now.[61] The administration's initial budget submission appears to agree, promising funding of $260 million for various intelligence-related purposes focused on state and local actors.[62]

PUBLIC ARENAS, SKYSCRAPERS, AND OTHER PROMINENT SITES

As noted above, about half of the nation's main stadiums and other large public arenas are partially protected against terrorism, whereas the other half are not. And with the exception of New York, but probably no other city, new buildings are not employing enough counterterrorism features.

One way to improve security within reasonable costs is to require that large buildings and public facilities carry terrorism insurance (and to require insurers to provide for such coverage, with a government backstop in the event of a catastrophic attack). Then the market can begin to establish a sense of best practices in the industry and offer correspondingly cheaper insurance rates to those implementing such procedures.[63] Unfortunately, this is not typically happening to date.[64]

Another option, employed in New York and certain other places, is to employ a combination of building code (as with New York City local law 33) and ongoing consultations between police and building owners, builders, and operators (especially to the extent that cities develop specialized counterterrorism capabilities within their police forces, as New York has done). This approach requires that local code be developed carefully, which is challenging and costly to builders at times, and also contentious. For example, in the city of New York today, there are ongoing questions about whether main structural supports are sufficiently resilient in new buildings. But many other aspects of code have been improved at reasonable cost, providing a model for other cities.

MILITARY AND NATIONAL GUARD CAPABILITIES

DoD's role in homeland security is often referred to as homeland defense. It is generally (and rightly) viewed as a supporting role, with actors such as FEMA, other parts of DHS, and state governors as the rightful lead agents for domestic emergencies.[65]

The Department of Defense has made major progress in homeland defense efforts, including planning for response to various types of catastrophes on American soil, trying to prevent such catastrophes through protection of infrastructure during alerts, and helping secure the nation's borders.[66] Two additional initiatives are still worth pursuing. First, a dedicated rapid-response National Guard brigade for domestic emergencies, available nationwide, makes sense. It would have higher readiness levels than most Guard units, since perhaps one battalion of the brigade would have to be on call at all times. Its average annual cost might reach $1 billion a year, especially at first (these costs are included in the DoD section of the summary table).[67]

In addition, more specialized small units may need to be created to fill out the three CCMERF teams now planned for handling certain kinds of attacks. There are small civil support teams in almost all states and territories for making initial assessments after any attack or other incident. In addition, there are now seventeen chemical, biological, radiological, nuclear, and high-yield explosive (CBRNE) enhanced response force packages (CERFPs). Each could handle a small incident on its own. But only one of the larger three CCMERF forces has even been notionally filled out with required forces (CCMERF means CBRNE Consequence Management Response Force). In addition to the general purpose response brigade, these more specialized capabilities are needed, with added costs perhaps in the range of $250 million a year.[68]

Second, procedures for helping the National Guard organize regionally, so that neighboring states may help each other more dependably and quickly in major crises, are still informal and fairly weak. They should be strengthened. Natural steps would include improving coordinated planning and creation of shared databases on available resources, as well as a new policy allowing governors to activate their own Guard units for deployment to neighboring states involuntarily (that is, without allowing the individual soldier to decline the opportunity to serve, if circumstances are severe enough). There is also a case for allowing governors to command and control the use of certain elements of the active duty military in case of domestic emergencies, when circumstances warrant.[69] Likely average costs would be under $100 million a year for such planning and preparations.

BIOLOGICAL SENSORS, NETWORKS, AND ANTIDOTES

Biological weapons threats are another dangerous matter for the country. There has been considerable progress, but many vulnerabilities remain.

Technology is often a limiting factor. For example, better detectors are being developed. However, they would usually pick up an agent only four hours after dispersal—and as of now even this capability is still in the development and testing stage.[70] That is an improvement to be sure, compared with the current capability, deployed in thirty cities, that involves a likely delay of ten to thirty-four hours between sampling and confirmation of an agent's presence at a laboratory.[71] But even getting to this four-hour capability requires adequate resources. Given the pace of progress, it seems doubtful that the federal government is investing enough in basic R&D to improve detector technology or in dissemination of sensors to provide whatever reasonable coverage is attainable.[72] Annual resourcing for biological and also for radiological detectors should probably increase in the range of $300 million, as a ballpark figure.

The nation's food supply is not particularly well secured. The likelihood of an al Qaeda attack against the food supply can be debated. But in keeping with the argument of an earlier Brookings study, it makes sense to beef up homeland security efforts in cases where there is at least a plausible counterterrorism case for doing so *and* a second, nonsecurity rationale. By many accounts, the nation's food supply is not safe against routine problems with bacteria in produce or with diseased meat or other such concerns. As such, increasing annual funding by roughly another $300 million for local food testing does make sense.[73] Alternatively, terrorism insurance could be required for food processing centers and for food distribution networks. The idea would be to have insurance companies incentivize firms to adopt best practices for site safety and security at fixed plants, and for drivers of vehicles, by offering better rates to those willing to take common-sense security steps.[74]

Addressing the future threat of biological pathogens is a daunting proposition. We have made progress in stockpiling antidotes to several diseases—smallpox, anthrax, plague. The Strategic National Stockpile has 60 million treatment courses of antibiotics for anthrax and pneumonic plague; it also has 300 million doses of smallpox vaccine.[75] But in general, we cannot respond effectively to threats that are impossible to specify in advance. Rather, we must try to create good early warning networks, rapid vaccine development and production capabilities, and effective dissemination networks for vaccines and antidotes. The latter might involve citizens' groups or perhaps postal workers delivering necessary vaccines or antidotes. Better electronic information systems could help individuals and families understand how to minimize their dangers and take precautions.[76]

Securing facilities where potent biological agents are present is still a challenging proposition. One reason is the increases in people working with such materials. About 15,000 individuals are now registered to work with biological agents.[77] According to the congressionally created Commission on the Prevention of Weapons of Mass Destruction and Terrorism, in its 2008 report, the facilities in which these individuals work are not regulated unless they receive federal grants or obtain certain pathogens.[78] The need for better oversight is increasingly an international challenge as well. Biological research is hardly confined to, or dominated by, the United States. As such, an additional aspect of biological security is the need to promote tougher international standards on security for sensitive facilities and on background checks for those working in them. This is just one example of where homeland security goes beyond the literal and physical protection of the homeland to include working with foreign partners to help them better secure their own countries, citizens, and critical assets.[79] There may not be major additional budgetary implications of sharing best security practices with foreign nations and groups, but it is an important imperative just the same. And on balance, these concerns do reinforce the argument for an increase in the resources of the Food and Drug Administration (FDA) of the magnitude suggested above so that it can ensure the safety of pharmaceuticals and other products entering the United States from abroad.[80]

CARGO CONTAINERS

For all the cargo that is now inspected, most arriving in the country by sea still is not. Some have suggested quite fundamental changes in container inspections. We could physically inspect every container, instead of the current rate (just 5 to 6 percent of containers arriving by sea). We could also employ technologies to track containers en route to this country, especially if the inspection process on which we were counting had already occurred before their departure for the United States.[81]

Such major changes would be very expensive and may not be warranted at present. However, some additional steps do make sense. More dependable screening of containers, as opposed to actual inspection, is still needed. Accomplishing this goal requires a higher percentage of firms participating in the Customs-Trade Partnership against Terrorism (C-TPAT) program as well as tighter standards on participating firms. Better radiation detectors still need to be developed too, for scanning containers. Neither current nor even likely next-generation technologies will be completely reliable, given the low radiation signatures of highly enriched uranium compared with background radiation, so we need to keep working at this issue through R&D.[82] The United States also needs to do a better job of helping Mexico inspect cargo going from the United States southward; cargo containers and vehicles making the trip south of the border provide many of the guns that have contributed to 5,000 drug war–related deaths per year in Mexico in recent times.[83] The combined cost of these efforts is likely in the range of $200 million to $300 million a year.

It is important to bear in mind the likely consequences for the economy of a terrorist attack that led virtually overnight to much tighter security measures for cargo and for passengers at land crossings as well. As Steve Flynn has convincingly argued, the country has an added incentive in tightening certain types of security measures carefully and efficiently over a period of years rather than risking a situation in which the immediate imposition of new standards after an attack leads to a prolonged economic slowdown. It is much easier to beef up inspection capacity gradually than to try to make up for lost time after an attack (or warning of a possible attack) has occurred, which makes it necessary to prevent the types of cross-border commerce that had been commonplace.[84]

DRIVER'S LICENSES AND ID, AND THE U.S.-VISIT PROGRAM

Standards for reliable identification are still too weak in some states, which need to make better use of biometric indicators and of digitization technologies for verifying proper ownership. This is an important, relatively inexpensive, and sound policy that is impeded at present only by concerns about privacy and states' rights. Those concerns should be aired out and accommodated to an extent, but the basic soundness of the recommendation is hard to challenge. Former secretary of homeland security Michael Chertoff was convincing when he stated that "I have yet to hear how it advances privacy to retain a system in which driver's licenses can be readily forged or counterfeited." Chertoff then went on to argue that the risk of identity theft is the true threat to privacy.[85]

Relatedly, fingerprinting foreigners not only as they enter but also as they leave the country has merit. It allows much better tracking of suspicious individuals and is an important complement to existing security improvements.[86] Congress accordingly needs to fund the U.S.-VISIT (U.S. Visitor and Immigrant Status Indicator Technology) program at the level requested, $400 million a year, to allow implementation of the overdue program to track departures of visitors. This system can help the United States know when people overstay their passports; can sometimes help authorities discern when people are leaving or entering illegally; and can, when necessary, help them learn more about individuals' patterns of movements within the United States.[87] The Obama administration's February 2009 budget adds $45 million for an expanded pilot project for tracking exits from the country, which is a step in the right direction.[88]

HAZARDOUS MATERIAL SHIPPING

Trucks carrying hazardous materials are not amply protected at all stages in their normal operations. Background checks are being done on drivers now, fairly comprehensively it would appear.[89] But more measures are still needed. Background checks on many individuals remain somewhat slow; creating more capacity for speedier background checks may cost

$25 million a year and should be funded.[90] As another example, for trucks carrying the most hazardous materials, GPS locators and automatic, remote-activated braking technology should be considered. These technologies have been deployed elsewhere (as a crime fighting measure in some cases) and cost in the low thousands of dollars per vehicle at most; if the government subsidized their employment by private industry, much could be done for under $100 million a year.

In addition, many municipalities and regions have not yet developed response or evacuation plans in the event that a chemical spill or terrorist attack might contaminate a large region.[91] Such measures are also needed for possible response to radiological or biological attack, yet have not been systematically pursued.

INTERNATIONAL PROGRAMS

In some cases, direct U.S. support for foreign or multilateral efforts to improve homeland security is appropriate. As noted above, while it may seem oxymoronic to talk about conducting homeland security efforts abroad, only through cooperation can the world's countries effectively monitor global flows of people, goods, and money—and only through cooperation can they effectively employ borders to spotlight activities that may be illicit or dangerous.

There are two particularly important ways in which U.S. financial assistance can contribute usefully to homeland security efforts conducted abroad. The first is to help poor countries that want to beef up their internal intelligence databases or employ biometrics in their identification and travel documents or improve airline security but cannot afford to do so. The second is in regard to international efforts to detect, or better yet deter, illicit development, movement, and use of dangerous materials or agents. The United States should in some cases help strengthen international agencies responsible for monitoring activities in a number of potentially dangerous areas of scientific research and of commerce—and pay its roughly 25 percent share of associated costs.

CONCLUSION

The federal government's current actual outlays of about $40 billion a year on homeland security reflect a huge increase over pre-9/11 norms.

More important, they are in the right ballpark for addressing current threats and needs. They allow, most of all, a national strategy emphasizing prevention of attacks through thorough intelligence work and data sharing, as well as selected preparations against possible attacks (especially catastrophic strikes causing potentially thousands of deaths or billions of dollars of damage). But certain additional initiatives with a combined annual cost of just over $2.5 billion, designed to redress remaining gaps and vulnerabilities in a way that meets cost-benefit criteria and focuses on preventive efforts as well as on activities providing secondary benefits beyond homeland security, should be seriously considered by the Obama administration.

CHAPTER SIX

HARD POWER IN THE STATE DEPARTMENT AND FOREIGN AID PROGRAMS

THE ROLE OF THE State Department and of foreign assistance programs in national security has always been important—and in recent years, it has become yet more crucial. For example, the basic stability of societies like nuclear-armed Pakistan is of enormous significance for U.S. security, and various types of aid and cooperation programs can be relevant for addressing these challenges. Assistance efforts also are important for improving the safety and security of nuclear arms, biological materials, and other dangerous technologies in many places. Even in military-led operations, stabilization and reconstruction activities by the State Department are central to mission success. From relief to reconstruction to development to establishment of the rule of law to other matters, activities in which the State Department or another civilian agency should presumably have the lead role are numerous, and critically important. In the words of Lt. Gen. William Caldwell, under whose name a new manual on stability operations was released in late 2008, "Military success alone will not be sufficient to prevail in this environment. To confront the challenges before us, we must strengthen the capacity of the other elements of national power, leveraging the full potential of our interagency partners."[1]

A starting point for implementing this type of vision, shared by Secretary of Defense Gates among others, is a better allocation of budgetary resources. Too often, after lip service by military proponents of foreign aid, budget battles are waged separately, with DoD personnel speaking to their respective committees and subcommittees on Capitol Hill, and those involved in diplomacy and foreign assistance to a different group—and the latter being much less successful than the former. In theory, OMB as well as the congressional budget committees provide some unified oversight and opportunity for creation of a cohesive plan for allocating resources. In practice, the 800-pound gorilla of the Pentagon dominates other agencies, even when it is not trying to do so, and its proponents on Capitol Hill enjoy huge natural advantages over those pushing diplomacy and related instruments of soft power. There will not be any easy, comprehensive fix to this situation. But it needs to be recognized, including by the president and his entire national security team as well as the director of the Office of Management and Budget. One corollary of this outlook is that the Pentagon's ongoing Quadrennial Defense Review should include substantial State Department input and representation—and that State should itself do such a review for its own purposes, with DoD representation.[2]

A major premise of the following analysis is that the inattentiveness to personnel that has occurred over the years in our diplomacy and aid efforts needs to be fundamentally reversed. This goes beyond simple additions of modest numbers of foreign service officers, a process that has belatedly begun. The number of countries in the world is greater than ever before; the number of complex humanitarian and stabilization missions is significant; the importance of local knowledge, and hands-on experience, is critical in a fast-moving world. As such it is a false economy to minimize, outsource, or trivialize the role of on-site expertise. Just as we work hard to maintain excellence and depth in the ranks of our military personnel, and view such people as our greatest asset, we must now do the same with the State Department and related institutions. I take a fairly cautious approach to recommending relatively modest increases, out of budgetary conservatism; if anything, the case exists for doing even more.

Before proceeding with a set of suggestions for greater funding for diplomacy and aid, it is important to note that, in certain ways, the Department of Defense is supporting the Department of State and related activities today. Most of these mechanisms are in regard to the conflicts in Iraq and Afghanistan, where DoD's help is focused on aiding ongoing military operations, or on smaller-scale counterterrorism cooperation in a modest group of countries. Examples include the following:

—Sections 1206, 1207, 1210 funding (named after the relevant sections of appropriations bills) that in recent years has allowed the Department of Defense to provide the State Department with amounts typically in the range of $100 million annually for activities such as training of foreign militaries[3]

—Commanders' Emergency Response Program (CERP) funds, by which the Department of Defense has spent several billion dollars in Iraq and Afghanistan to spur job creation and economic activity at the direction of battlefield commanders in response to immediate needs in their sectors of operations[4]

—Supplemental funding for the Iraqi and Afghan security forces, which has averaged more than $5 billion a year for half a decade[5]

These types of programs, and this funding flexibility, have been sensible as a quick response to immediate needs. Some object to the role of the Department of Defense in such activities, which would seem more appropriate as State Department or aid efforts. (CERP funds effectively fund development activities, and funding for the Iraqi and Afghan security forces resembles Foreign Military Financing and International Military Education and Training programs, which are budgetarily controlled by State.) But this objection is not convincing to me. Training a foreign military with which the United States is actively involved in ongoing wartime operations is unambiguously a military activity, and while oversight is important, there is little point in trying to pretend that this is fundamentally a civilian activity; it is not. CERP projects have been rather effective on balance and allow those on the scene to respond immediately to population needs that are relevant not only for development but for helping protect U.S. uniformed personnel. No one should confuse what is happening in these places with normal development, and there is little risk of the model being applied to places where the U.S. military is not heavily engaged on the ground. Sections 1206, 1207, 1210 provisions reflect the Pentagon's awareness that, where possible, it should involve State and traditional development agencies.

However, even if these programs are generally sound, the broader question remains: how should the normal, non-war-related tools of the

State Department be strengthened for other types of activities when immediate wartime operations are not under way?

In addition to expanding resources for aid and diplomacy, other steps are needed too. For years the Pentagon has carried out a quadrennial defense review process. That should now become, or be complemented by, a quadrennial national security review. Integrating these two efforts could go a long way toward a better allocation of resources—and more collective, cogent lobbying by the entire executive branch for the resulting budget plan. To assist in this effort, a recent proposal to create a deputy national security advisor for interagency planning and resource allocation makes sense. In addition, as suggested by Cindy Williams and Gordon Adams, Congress should hold at least some budget hearings that consider all tools of foreign policy together.[6]

In that spirit, this book now turns to the *hard power tools* of the State Department and foreign assistance budgets—collectively known as the 150 federal budget function. These hard power instruments of 150 policy are defined here, somewhat subjectively, as those with direct and near-term security relevance such as security aid and the Office of Stabilization and Reconstruction at the State Department.

Of course, longer-term economic and human development is clearly of crucial importance for promoting peace and stability as well; poorer countries are unquestionably more prone to conflict, including conflicts that spill over into neighboring states.[7] As such, the case for increasing international development aid in such areas as education, agricultural assistance, and food aid is strong, and increases in total international resources of at least $30 billion to $40 billion a year (roughly one-quarter of which might be the U.S. share) should be considered. (This would correspond to roughly a 50 percent increase relative to current levels of effort.)[8] Economic aid to help developing countries adopt more environmentally friendly and low-carbon-emission technologies will also be appropriate in the coming years.[9] But basic economic and human development is not my main area of expertise and not the main scope of this study. That said, there are some cases in which economic aid has such direct and near-term implications for security, as with aid to Pakistan and a few other countries, that it is discussed below.

Before proceeding to specific suggestions, a few more words of background are in order. The foreign affairs, or 150, budget, which totaled about $40 billion a year at the end of the Bush administration, can be

TABLE 6-1. Main Categories of Spending in the 150 Budget[a]

By Main Category, as a Percentage of the Total	
Development and Humanitarian Aid	33
State Department Operations	19
Military Aid	13
International and Multilateral Organizations	13
Security and Economic Aid	10
Narcotics Interdiction and Prevention	4
Food Aid	3
Public Diplomacy	3
Other	2
By Specific Line Items of Direct Security Relevance, Millions of Dollars[b]	
Civilian Stabilization Initiative	250
Broadcasting	730
Economic Support Fund	3,150
Eastern Europe and Baltic States Fund	275
Independent States of the Former Soviet Union	350
International Narcotics and Law Enforcement	1,200
Andean Counterdrug Initiative	405
Migration and Refugee Assistance	765
Nonproliferation, Antiterrorism, and Demining	500
International Military Education and Training	90
Foreign Military Financing	4,810
International Peacekeeping Assessment	1,500
Peacekeeping Operations (additional)	250

Source: Susan B. Epstein and Kennon H. Nakamura, "State, Foreign Operations, and Related Programs: FY2009 Appropriations" (Washington: Congressional Research Service, August 21, 2008), pp. 5, 30–35.

a. 2009 foreign affairs budget request.

b. Rounded.

broken down into the following categories and approximate budget allocations. The main categories considered here concern military aid, security and economic aid, public diplomacy, narcotics, and State Department operations (see table 6-1).[10]

For historical perspective, it is also worth noting the major bilateral recipients of American aid in recent years; two separate lists are provided, one for 2008 and one for the 2009 budget request as submitted to Congress by the Bush administration (see table 6-2).[11]

The Obama administration has requested a substantial increase in 150 funding for 2010, with an increase in discretionary budget authority from

TABLE 6-2. Top Recipients of U.S. Foreign Aid[a]

	2009 Request
Israel	2.55
Egypt	1.50
Afghanistan	1.05
Pakistan	0.83
South Africa	0.58
Kenya	0.57
Colombia	0.54
Jordan	0.53
Mexico	0.50
Nigeria	0.49
	2008 Budget
Afghanistan	2.79
Israel	2.38
Egypt	1.70
Iraq	1.56
Jordan	0.94
Pakistan	0.80
Kenya	0.59
South Africa	0.57
Colombia	0.54
Nigeria	0.49
Ethiopia	0.46

Source: Susan B. Epstein and Kennon H. Nakamura, "State, Foreign Operations, and Related Programs: FY2009 Appropriations" (Washington: Congressional Research Service, August 21, 2008), p. 20.

a. All types of bilateral aid, in billions of dollars. Not all funds from supplemental appropriations are included here.

$47.2 billion to $51.7 billion; that $47.2 billion figure for 2009 itself represented a major increase from the $40.9 billion level of 2008.[12] Initial reaction from Congress has not been favorable to this proposed increase. (For updates, see www.stimson.org, as this book is going to press in early May.) This proposed increase reflects attention to many of the same issues and priorities that I address below, most notably increased aid for Afghanistan and Pakistan as well as strengthening of the nation's foreign service officer corps for both diplomacy and development.[13] As with previous sections on the defense budget, my recommendations are independent of the Obama administration's, but similarly motivated.

We now turn to an examination of several foreign policy instruments meriting reinvigoration and increased resources.

Cooperative Threat Reduction with Other Countries

No instrument of foreign policy and foreign assistance can be more crucial to the nation's security than efforts to ensure the safety and security of nuclear weapons and other dangerous materials around the world. Indeed, few instruments of defense policy can be comparably important.

Since 1992, the United States has spent about $15 billion to help Russia and other countries secure their nuclear capabilities, dismantle excess capabilities, employ former weapons scientists in benign pursuits, and otherwise reduce the risk of nuclear proliferation and other threats from weapons of mass destruction. Much has been accomplished. But much still has to be done, in regard to not only nuclear technologies but biological and chemical ones as well.

As underscored by Graham Allison of Harvard and other scholars, the world needs to move toward a *Fort Knox* standard of nuclear security, by which is meant that plutonium and enriched uranium would be guarded just as securely as gold is today, everywhere they are found in the world.[14] Of course, unlike the case with gold, that means reducing those materials to their minimally acceptable levels. But it also means securing whatever remains very robustly.

Several steps are needed to achieve this:

—A continuation of improved safeguards at those sites in Russia lacking them (though Russia clearly has the means to pay for such efforts itself now), something that might be pursued through the next round of arms control (which could, among other things, consolidate and reduce tactical warhead stocks)[15]

—Convincing more countries to modify research reactors running on highly enriched uranium (HEU) to use lower-enriched uranium fuel that, if stolen, is not usable in bombs

—Helping countries test their security procedures at nuclear plants through exercises and other on-site inspection procedures

—Funding any resulting remedial security measures for countries not able to do so themselves

—Buying more excess enriched uranium to make it unavailable to those who would want it for nefarious purposes

—Encouraging countries to create research consortia involving nuclear reactors so that excess reactors for such purposes can be shut down and remaining ones better protected (even when HEU is no longer used as a fuel source, the reactors are sensitive sites, since they still contain fuel that can be turned into weapons-grade fissile material and they still contain waste usable in dirty bombs)

A detailed analysis by Anthony Wier and Matthew Bunn suggests that up to several hundred million dollars a year in added United States funding may be sensible for these types of efforts, on top of the amounts typically spent by the U.S. government in recent years for cooperative nuclear threat reduction programs. In particular, for each of the above types of efforts, sustained programmatic increases on the order of $50 million a year seem sound and within the capacity of relevant agencies to utilize effectively.[16] Initiatives should also be included for blending down reactor fuel globally, helping Pakistan better secure its nuclear facilities and better monitor its security personnel (using redundant personnel as needed, including extra or separate groups of guards), improving research on nuclear forensics so any terrorist use of nuclear materials can be more easily investigated, and improving security procedures at existing sites. On balance, a net increase of about $400 million a year is sensible and consistent with the basic budgetary, strategic, and political constraints at play.[17]

A previous study by a congressionally mandated task force on the United Nations devised several overlapping or parallel recommendations, starting with nuclear issues but extending to chemical and biological matters as well.[18] Most of these kinds of initiatives are not particularly expensive; the total price tag for the United States would be in the range of $100 million a year. To be more specific:[19]

—a roster of biological technology experts should be created, trained to carry out key procedures in a standard and uniform way, and paid a modest stipend to be on call should suspicious activity that might violate the Biological Weapons Convention occur somewhere in the world;

—standards for safety at biological research facilities around the world should be created, best practices encouraged, and collegial inspections conducted to offer advice for improvements in some cases;

—the Organization for the Prohibition of Chemical Weapons should develop capacities to advise countries on how to better secure and protect their chemical plants against sabotage or theft of sensitive materials;

—the International Atomic Energy Agency should be accorded greater resources for investigating nuclear trafficking and for carrying out the inspections needed under the so-called Additional Protocol.

CORE DIPLOMACY

Anyone who has watched U.S. diplomats help convince countries like Ukraine to give up their nuclear weapons after the Soviet Union dissolved, or help Iraqi politicians develop realism and pragmatism in building their new democracy, or negotiate nuclear arms control arrangements for enhancing nonproliferation efforts around the world, or work with allies to put pressure on Iran over its nuclear program will likely appreciate the direct and immediate role of diplomacy in promoting U.S. national security.

Yet budgetary resources do not reflect this reality. After the cold war, the United States cut back on its foreign service funding even as new embassies were required in the new states of the former Yugoslavia and former Soviet Union. That trend has since been reversed, but gaps remain nonetheless. A larger menu of global issues, more countries and multilateral organizations to work with, greater requirements for staffing in areas such as visa processing, and a clear need to promote America's image around the world leave numerous unmet needs. In addition, the language skills of the foreign service remain deficient, with acute shortfalls of several hundred people in languages such as Arabic. Other training needs go unaddressed as well.

A recent task force composed of members from the American Academy of Diplomacy and the Stimson Center documented gaps in all these areas and calculated needs accordingly. Its recommendations for another 1,100 staff members for core diplomacy, above the 6,000 or so now employed, and nearly 1,300 more personnel to allow ongoing training and professional development are convincing and worth the recommended $1 billion a year in total costs.[20] (A more ambitious proposal by Bruce Jones, Carlos Pascual, and Stephen Stedman would envision doubling the U.S. Foreign Service within a decade. This larger goal may be worth pursuing itself.[21]) Such increases would have numerous, very tangible benefits. For example, they would allow the foreign service to pursue mid-career education opportunities for its officers akin to what the Department of Defense provides for its senior leaders.[22] They would also allow better preparation of foreign service officers for their roles in provincial reconstruction teams, as discussed below.[23]

PUBLIC DIPLOMACY

At a time of prevalent anti-Americanism around the world, the roles of public diplomacy and democracy promotion have tangible security importance themselves. This type of work is somewhat tangential to war fighting, admittedly, and is usually placed under the heading of *soft power* rather than hard. However, in light of the need to address the recruiting efforts of terrorist organizations around the world, based as they often are on perceptions about the United States, I have elected to include a short summary of programs worthy of additional resources here. The interruption of the recruitment of the next generation of extremists may use political and mental tools, but it is a direct response to a clear and present danger.

Certain news services like Radio Sawa and Alhurra TV have been created and reasonably well resourced in recent years. However, some traditional broadcasting services have been scaled back. For example, services have been reduced to parts of central and eastern Europe. Given the fragility of some relatively young democracies, and ongoing tensions in the Caucasus region and elsewhere, this is a mistake. Growth in new programs should not generally come at the expense of traditional ones. Initiatives in much of south and central Asia where Arabic is not spoken are needed too. The overall reduction in total public diplomacy by nearly one-quarter since the cold war ended is a false economy. A spending increase of about $400 million in the annual budget is warranted.[24]

In addition to this support for actual broadcasting, Kristin Lord has suggested several important new ideas designed to enhance the United States' broader image in the world and understanding of the world. They include a tripling of Fulbright fellows to 10,000 a year and creation of web resources providing information in multiple languages on key issues to developing countries, such as agricultural and primary health care practices. Web resources should also facilitate efforts by U.S. officials, scholars, and others to communicate with the rest of the world. Programs like Fulbright scholarships should make greater efforts to encourage U.S. students to study in the developing world and should also try to encourage more U.S. minority students to participate.[25] Related ideas would have the United States open Internet cafes and other such minicenters around the world. Juan Cole has further suggested greater efforts to translate great works of literature and political thought into English from Arabic, and vice versa, and disseminate these widely, so that fewer Americans and overseas Muslims form their respective views about each other from the unrepresentative words of extremists or polemicists.[26] The additional cost could be roughly $400 million a year.[27]

Such efforts will not, of course, solve the problem of Arab (and other) political reform. As Tamara Wittes reminds us, "Until American democracy assistance programs engage the most powerful tools the United States can bring to bear—namely, its diplomatic and economic relations with Arab governments—all the small-bore programs in the world will not do the job." Yet there are a number of areas where small-bore programs in promoting democracy, improving the American image abroad, helping strengthen technical proficiency in key governments, and other such measures can help.[28]

STABILIZATION AND RECONSTRUCTION EFFORTS AND THE STATE DEPARTMENT

The United States has, starting after Vietnam and accelerating after the cold war, neglected its tools for helping other countries develop economically and stabilize themselves after conflict. Fairly dramatic measures are now called for to compensate, including even the idea of creating a new department in the government headed by a cabinet member and devoted to development and stabilization.

Since 1980, the Agency for International Development's workforce has dropped from 4,000 to 2,200 employees, roughly, leaving it more and more as a contracting force rather than a field development agency. (The drop is even more staggering when measured against the Vietnam-era peak strength of 15,000.[29]) It has also been brought into the State Department, not necessarily the right answer given the long-term perspectives required of development practitioners.[30]

Whatever happens on the organizational side, more resources are needed. My focus here, given the hard power focus of this section, is on conflict environments, and most specifically the concept of provincial reconstruction teams (or PRTs, often embedded within military units). These are not the only ways in which field resources will be deployed and

used, of course. There are other ways in which the added capacity proposed below might be deployed. PRTs will generally not be needed if
security environments are relatively benign, for example. So some of the
personnel discussed below might deploy in more traditional missions as
well as be available for PRT assignments. But the recent PRT experience
is used here as a means of estimating the likely need for future capacity
nonetheless.

The need for U.S. field workers who are focused on economic recovery and development has grown substantially in recent years, especially
in Iraq and Afghanistan but also in other places. There are about twenty
to thirty provincial reconstruction teams in each of these two countries;
each typically includes from a few dozen to 100 or more individuals.[31]
These PRTs help create local jobs and also help mentor local capacity for
carrying out economic development projects; they have on the whole
been successful.[32] But they also underscore the need for increased capacity. Either Iraq or Afghanistan can require 1,000 development experts for
hard power missions. Not all of these need be American, or even civilian. Indeed, in Iraq, many of the Americans in PRTs are military personnel (or individuals from specialized agencies of the government or even
land grant colleges and the like back in the United States). And in
Afghanistan in particular, many team members are non-American. But as
one way of gauging requirements in the future, a starting point might be
the assumption that we will need as many PRT personnel from the
United States alone as are now deployed in Iraq and Afghanistan from
all countries—and that these people should *all* be civilians, ideally. Neither of these assumptions is likely to be completely correct or necessary,
but future missions could also be larger than those in Iraq and
Afghanistan. Again, these assumptions are not meant to suggest that
PRTs in general, or the current concept for PRTs in Iraq and Afghanistan
in particular, must always be the mechanism by which civil-military
efforts are coordinated in conflict zones or that all development personnel must formally be within the PRT. But for estimating necessary overall capacity, this model is useful.

Military personnel can certainly carry out some PRT tasks, and military protection is often essential for PRTs to function well in war-torn
lands in any event—lending support to the idea of *embedded PRTs*
(ePRTs) that are deployed within a battalion or brigade. But many functions conducted by PRTs and other stabilization and reconstruction

experts are simply too specialized to expect military personnel to be the main agents in charge of such activities. Restoring the rule of law, police forces, and criminal justice systems are among the most challenging tasks that are, naturally, rather alien to military cultures. Ironically, given its pragmatic approach to problems, the U.S. military often winds up doing things well that it might not be expected to. For example, its Commanders' Emergency Response Program funds have often been more effective than large-scale contractor-led development efforts in Iraq, since the former can be employed in modest amounts and without the requirements that U.S. contractors be employed and U.S. goods purchased using these funds. But a pragmatic civilian corps with the same type of approach and attitude would be better yet.[33] Moreover, as of 2005, even the Bush administration (which had put the Pentagon in charge of all aspects of the Iraq war, even after Saddam was overthrown) recognized that the State Department should be the lead agency in reconstruction and stabilization missions, via its National Security Presidential Directive (NSPD) 44.[34]

Scaling from these missions, and recognizing that other missions could occur as well, it seems reasonable to try to create capacity to deploy up to 2,000 American civilians for PRTs and related activities at a time. Since these missions can endure, a rotation base of individuals is needed. Some could be full-time employees of the Office of Stabilization and Reconstruction, others could be designees from other parts of government, while others could be the equivalent of military reservists. The latter individuals, like military reservists, would be paid and undergo periodic training; they would then be obliged to deploy if called upon to do so (as would individuals from other federal agencies who signed up for the program and received its benefits).[35]

This type of logic leads to a broad requirement in the range of 10,000 such individuals for development and reconstruction efforts in conflict and post-conflict zones. Assuming a mix of active and reserve individuals, the standing annual cost would be about $1 billion.[36] Other estimates, done with greater specificity and detail, come to similar conclusions about the need for more capacity, as well as more training.[37] For example, an American Academy of Diplomacy and Stimson Center task force proposed an increase of 1,050 foreign service officers at the U.S. Agency for International Development (USAID), as well as 200 civil servants, and more than 500 direct-hire staff in the specific domain of stabilization and reconstruction, with a total cost of just over $800 million annually.[38] A somewhat more modest proposal by the founding director of the State Department's Office of Stabilization and Reconstruction would fund 250 direct-hire, full-time employees for these purposes while also creating a standby force (designees for rapid deployment from various parts of government) and a reserve force (akin to military reserves). It might cost on the order of $350 million a year.[39] In fact, the Bush administration wound up requesting something similar in its 2009 budget submission, at a cost of about $250 million, but it is not at all clear that Congress will be supportive of this idea anytime soon. (The $250 million included $75 million for 250 full-time personnel for an interagency Active Response Corps as well as 2,000 people already working in other parts of government who would join a standby response corps, $85 million for a 2,000-person civilian reserve corps, $65 million for any initial deployment costs, and $25 million for the Office of the Coordinator for Reconstruction and Stabilization.)[40] And a recent RAND study proposes 5,000 more personnel.[41]

OTHER COUNTRIES

Without going into detail on a case-by-case basis, there is a general need to have extra funds ready for propitious moments in a peace process when modest sums can do a great deal of good. After all, the successful "clear, hold, build" philosophy used in the surge in Iraq required rapid improvement of quality of life right after key security operations, to show populations the value of working for peace and working with their own government as well as with the international community. The same principle applies elsewhere. Here I simply sketch out possible added needs to estimate how many additional resources might be required. My goal is primarily to gain a sense of how much larger aid budgets should be and less to argue for a concrete new initiative for a given country.

The basic theme here favors more Economic Support Funds, a key foreign aid tool of the U.S. government. Within this account, the 2009 request for the Congo was a very modest $40 million a year, for example, and for Somalia, $20 million. The West Bank and Gaza, after receiving hundreds of millions in 2008, were to receive only $75 million in 2009, as the role of Hamas in much of the Palestinian regions precluded any great spirit of generosity out of Washington—and the Gaza Strip conflict of December–January 2008–09 will not likely change this situation. But these are precisely the sorts of situations where, depending on the evolution of events, more money could quickly be appropriated (for example, to strengthen Palestinian groups besides Hamas, such as Fatah). At least $200 million a year in added funding is appropriate.

Any peace deal in the Middle East would likely lead to quick congressional support of a large aid package. Although Hamas's rule over the Gaza Strip complicates enormously the attempt to help build infrastructure and the foundations for economic growth among the Palestinian people, this set of objectives remains crucial.[42] In the coming years, the peace process may make it possible to pursue them more assertively. At that point, an additional major program funding initiative will be needed, as part of an international effort, to help produce major and tangible benefits for the Palestinian people to counter the inevitable efforts of rejectionists. A corresponding U.S. share might be $250 million a year or so once interim measures are complete, and at least $1 billion a year once a true two-state solution is negotiated—given that the estimated costs of a major development initiative for the Palestinians could reach $35 billion (I am assuming it would be carried out over roughly a ten-year period).[43]

However, short-term responses for other states could be just as important—and less likely to command immediate congressional attention. Thankfully, they would also typically demand much more modest amounts of money to help consolidate any peace deal. African states in particular tend not to receive much publicity, or rapid additional funding, even when circumstances suggest they should. This fact bolsters the case for another $100 million to $300 million in unallocated ESF funds for quick use by the executive branch should circumstances seem appropriate. The amounts are modest enough that Congress would not be giving up a large amount of budgetary control.[44] Somewhat larger amounts of money could be needed, too, for the unlikely but not impossible scenario of a broader North Korea deal involving arms control, nuclear disarmament by Pyongyang, and economic reform facilitated by the global community.[45]

The Merida Initiative to help Mexico counter drug trafficking, totaling a $1.4 billion commitment, is a good concept. It seeks to help strengthen Mexican law enforcement and judicial institutions, as is appropriate.[46] But it is disbursing money too slowly. It is not clear that more money is required—though it may be. What is clear is that a process taking nearly a year to disburse 2 percent of initial funds ($7 million out of $400 million in the first installment of aid) is not being handled with wartime urgency. Yet Mexico is facing serious challenges. In 2008, adjusted for population, it lost as many people from drug-related violence as Afghanistan lost from its war. Expedited bureaucratic procedures must be found to accelerate this process.[47]

A final area in which modest amounts of added funding might make sense is the Kimberley Process, to legitimate the origins of diamonds to reduce the risks that the diamond trade will inadvertently fund warlords and militias around the world. If more resources are needed for this process, above the very modest $1 million to $3 million a year recently allocated, they should be provided.[48]

AID TO AFGHANISTAN

Given their importance, several countries merit a few additional words of discussion and a rough estimate of additional required aid resources, even if a detailed examination of these cases is beyond my present scope.

Afghanistan is clearly a crucial country in question. And one very important aspect of the current Afghanistan mission that needs rethinking, as well as more resources, concerns the Afghan security forces. For several years after the U.S.-led overthrow of the Taliban in Afghanistan in 2001, the United States and its partners sought to create only a modestly sized Afghan army and police force. The logic was that Afghanistan could not afford a larger force on its own, and any force built by the international community should be self-sustainable even after foreign actors and donors had left the scene sometime in the coming years.[49]

This logic is flawed. In fact, the United States has given generous aid to Israel and Egypt at the level of $2 billion to $3 billion a year for decades; it has done so for substantial stretches for the Republic of Korea, Taiwan, the Palestinian Authority, and other states as well. There is no reason it cannot commit to doing so for Afghanistan.

Afghanistan's security forces are now slated to grow to some 216,000 (134,000 soldiers and 82,000 police), after being in the range of 125,000 in recent years. Reaching the higher figure will take time, given the dearth of Western trainers available for the job, but even that number is too low. Afghanistan needs a security force that approaches that of Iraq in size, given that it is comparably populous and even bigger in land area. In fact, a force close to half a million (between army and police) may be the right target. Once a training program ramps up, it may be possible to recruit (or conscript) and train nearly 100,000 soldiers and police a year, if Iraq is a model. If such an Afghan security force costs the international community $5 billion a year, with roughly a third coming from the United States, it is still a good deal compared with the likely alternative. Indeed, start-up costs could be higher as equipment is purchased in large amounts, but with a mission costing the international community some $4 billion a month militarily at present, these assistance costs need to be kept in perspective. As such, the United States should envision adding $1 billion a year to its security aid for Afghanistan.

As for economic aid, there are several broad problems. One is clearly the difficulty of getting money to the grassroots level; most U.S. development funds come with too many stipulations about the percentage of monies that must be spent on American personnel or services. In a wartime environment, this is even less justifiable than is normally the case with development aid. Although using the military more in development is *not* the right basic approach, the military's flexibility in spending so-called Commanders' Emergency Response Program funds is a better model than most others, and this model should be emulated.[50] Greater emphasis on agriculture, an employment-creating development effort, is also appropriate. If done well so as to include the creation of infrastructure to get crops to market and get fertilizer and seeds to farmers, it can also serve as one of the most effective types of counternarcotics strategy. According to Bruce Riedel, the scale of most major efforts in Afghanistan to date in areas such as education and road building has been roughly one-fourth to one-half of what is needed, suggesting at least a doubling in the pace of economic development activities so that some major results are achieved within several years. An added effort in the range of another $700 million a year would seem appropriate.[51] That effort should also attempt to create a multiyear plan for completing key goals (rather than revisiting interim goals yearly). It should also place greater emphasis on developing regional and indigenous firms for tasks like road building rather than relying so heavily on Western organizations and companies.[52]

Aid to Pakistan

Having averaged more than $1.5 billion a year since September 11, U.S. assistance to Pakistan has been a crucial tool in the war on terror.

However, until recently, that aid has been used largely for macroeconomic priorities such as balance of payments support and for traditional military priorities of Pakistan's armed forces focused largely on conventional operations and deterrence (especially vis-à-vis India). These priorities have done little to deal with insurgency, lawlessness, and extremism in the Federally Administered Tribal Areas (FATA)—the region that provides sanctuary for many resistance fighters in Afghanistan and that also threatens nuclear-armed Pakistan's own internal stability. A substantial amount of money—up to $6 billion or so—has been directed to the FATA in theory. But only $40 million of that, according to GAO, has gone for true development activities. Almost all has gone to the Pakistani security forces for operations of uncertain competence and commitment in that region (and it is not clear that all those funds have truly been spent there).[53] Funds for equipment optimized for counterinsurgency, such as Cobra attack helicopters, have often been redirected or delayed.[54]

Some advocate demanding that Pakistan simply change its priorities for spending U.S. aid, away from conventional military modernization and toward training and equipping of Pakistan's Frontier Corps. They also favor demanding greater educational, infrastructural, and economic development support for remote regions around the country out of existing aid funds. These individuals may be right in theory, but they are probably wrong in practice, given Pakistani politics.[55] It would be a mistake to insist that Islamabad simply redirect U.S. funds to such pursuits, because Pakistan's own priorities are different. The more realistic hope is to offer additional aid, at least at the level the Obama administration appears to envision—tripling development aid while adding about half a billion dollars a year in military assistance—provided that it is properly employed in activities that help stabilize and develop the country's northwest regions.[56] To be sure, Pakistan can be encouraged to shift more of its own funds to appropriate activities—as it may now be doing with greater emphasis on training and equipping the Frontier Corps, better salaries and other benefits for the nation's police, and more effort to enlist the so-called lashkars or tribal militias from frontier provinces in security efforts.[57] If it does so, U.S. aid might be increased even further, as an incentive and a reward. But we should not delay needed efforts in Pakistan's west over a budgetary showdown with Islamabad that we may well lose.

CHAPTER SEVEN

CONCLUSION

THE UNITED STATES NEEDS to fund all its tools of foreign policy and national security. The times demand it, with two ongoing wars in Iraq and Afghanistan; ongoing nuclear challenges in Iran, Pakistan, and North Korea; a resurgent power in the form of Russia; a growing power in the form of China; an unresolved Mideast peace process; and numerous other challenges to U.S. and global security interests.

Yet at the same time, the United States must budget frugally. Historians and political scientists are right to remind us all that economically weak countries cannot remain great powers. The recent economic crisis underscores this core reality. While it is no time to slash budgets recklessly—and, indeed, while it would likely be counterproductive to do so even on economic grounds—the nation needs a robust national security toolkit at the most reasonable cost possible.

Many will disagree with my specific suggestions here; others will see them as too modest in scale or scope. But they are motivated by the above, underlying philosophy—a recognized need for fiscal prudence, combined with an awareness of the nation's national security requirements for the complex challenges of the world today. They are guided less by a fundamentally new worldview than by careful scrutiny of specific programs, with an eye to preparing and equipping the country's foreign policy establishment for the Obama era. The resulting budget proposal is more or less spending neutral, adding roughly as much to 150 and homeland security as it takes from 050. However, it does not include funding for new antipoverty or energy initiatives that are beyond my scope. Nor does it include any estimate of war costs, now nearly $200 billion a year, which are likely to decline substantially more than any antipoverty and energy costs grow in the first term of the Obama presidency. All things considered, the price tag is quite modest, and would in fact allow the nation's national security costs as a percentage of GDP to decline modestly in the coming years. It should be well within our reach and our means.

Appendix

FIGURE A-1. U.S. Air Force Annual Rate of Aerial Mishaps[a]

Mishaps per 100,000 flying hours

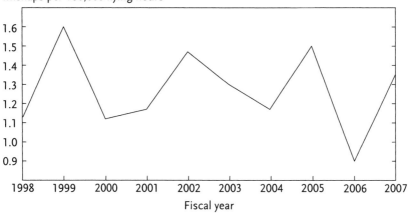

Fiscal year

Source: "2008 USAF Almanac," *Air Force* (May 2008), p. 65.
a. Includes loss of life, permanent total disability, destroyed aircraft, or more than $1 million in property damages.

TABLE A-1. U.S. Air Force Active Duty Inventory
(as of September 30, 2007)

Type	Total aircraft inventory	Primary aircraft inventory[a]
Bomber		
B-1	67	51
B-2	21	16
B-52	85	54
Total	173	121
Fighter/Attack		
A-10	125	113
OA-10A	71	54
F-15A-D	292	246
F-15E	223	189
F-16	700	588
F-22A	97	85
F-117	44	28
Total	1,552	1,303
Helicopter		
HH-60	68	53
UH-1	92	53
Total	160	106
Reconnaissance/BM/C3I		
E-3	32	27
E-4	4	3
EC-130	14	10
MQ-1	131	111
MQ-9	13	0
NC-135	1	0
OC-135	2	2
RC-135	22	17
RQ-4	12	9
U-2	33	29
WC-135	2	1
Total	266	209
Special OPS forces		
AC-130	25	19
CV-22	7	0
MC-130	46	40
MH-53	22	19
Total	100	78

Type	Total aircraft inventory	Primary aircraft inventory[a]
Tanker		
HC-130	19	19
KC-10	59	54
KC-135	199	176
Total	277	249
Trainer		
T-1	179	141
T-6	320	203
T-37	87	87
T-38	462	381
T-41	4	4
T-43	8	7
T-51	3	3
TC-135	3	2
Glider	42	26
UV-18	3	2
Total	1,111	856
Transport		
C-5	33	33
C-12	28	27
C-17	153	111
C-20	10	10
C-21	38	32
C-32	4	4
C-37	9	6
C-40	4	1
C-130	173	156
VC-25	2	2
Total	454	382
Total Air Force active duty	4,093	3,304

Source: "2008 USAF Almanac," *Air Force* (May 2008), p. 60.
a. That is, those in the force structure of operational units.

TABLE A-2. Age of Active Duty Aircraft Fleet for U.S. Air Force
(as of September 30, 2007)

Type	0–3	3–6	6–9	9–12	12–15	15–18	18–21	21–24	24+	Total	Average
A-10								11	185	196	25.8
B-1B							66	1		67	20.1
B-2			7	10	3	1				21	13.1
B-52									85	85	45.8
C-5							26	5	2	33	20.9
C-10						1	11	30	17	29	22.7
C-12							4	8	16	28	27.3
C-17	35	42	33	20	19	4				153	6.6
C-20				1	1		8			10	18.7
C-21								38		38	22.7
C-25					2					2	16.9
C-32			2	2						4	9.0
C-37		3	6							9	6.7
C-40	2	2								4	3.6
C-130	10	1	1		15	20	16	5	209	277	33.0
C-135									229	229	45.6
CV-22	7									7	1.1
E-3								3	29	32	27.8
E-4									4	4	33.3
F-15C-D						1	66	84	141	292	23.9
F-15E		10	16		35	114	48			223	15.5
F-16	1	13	16	19	178	301	90	81	1	700	16.3
F-22	74	22	1							97	2.1
F-117						5	12	20	7	44	21.5
H-1									92	92	36.4
H-53									22	22	36.7
H-60			5	1	5	38	10	1	8	68	17.4
Q-1	131									131	1.5
Q-4	9	3								12	2.0
Q-9	9	4								12	2.0
T-1				57	101	21				179	12.9
T-6	161	125	34							320	3.2
T-37									87	87	42.7
T-38									462	462	40.2
T-41									4	4	38.1
T-43									8	8	33.4
T-51	3									3	2.1
U-2						1	8	12	12	33	24.2
UV-18				1					2	3	23.5
Glider		40	1		1					42	5.2
Total	442	265	115	108	365	511	366	299	1,622	4,093	23.1
Percent	11	7	3	3	9	13	9	7	40		

Source: "2008 USAF Almanac," *Air Force* (May 2008), p. 61.

TABLE A-3. U.S. Air Force Reserve Command Inventory

(as of September 30, 2007)

Type	Total aircraft inventory	Primary aircraft inventory[a]
Bomber		
B-52	9	8
Fighter/Attack		
A-10	44	38
OA-10A	7	3
F-16	53	48
Total	104	89
Helicopter		
HH-60	15	13
Reconnaissance/BM/C3I		
WC-130	17	10
Special Ops Forces		
MC-130	14	8
Tanker		
HC-130	5	5
KC-135	80	72
Total	85	77
Transport		
C-5	45	40
C-9	3	3
C-17	8	8
C-40	2	0
C-130	94	92
Total	152	143
Total Air Force Reserve Command	396	348

Source: "2008 USAF Almanac," *Air Force* (May 2008), p. 60.
a. That is, those in the force structure of operational units.

TABLE A-4. Age of U.S. Air Force Reserve Command Fleet
(as of September 30, 2007)

Type	0–3	3–6	6–9	9–12	12–15	15–18	18–21	21–24	24+	Total	Average
A-10								1	50	51	27.0
B-52									9	9	45.5
C-5							15	1	29	45	30.2
C-9									3	3	32.5
C-17	8									8	1.9
C-40	2									2	0.4
C-130	7	7	4	6	18	12	24	8	44	130	22.0
C-135									80	80	46.3
F-16						1	50	2		53	19.8
H-60						15				15	16.7
Total	17	7	4	6	18	28	89	12	215	396	28.1
Percent	4	2	1	2	5	7	22	3	54		

Source: "2008 USAF Almanac," *Air Force* (May 2008), p. 62.

TABLE A-5. U.S. Air National Guard Inventory
(as of September 30, 2007)

Type	Total aircraft inventory	Primary aircraft inventory[a]
Fighter/Attack		
A-10	78	78
OA-10A	28	18
F-15A-D	145	91
F-16	495	422
Total	746	609
Helicopter		
HH-60	81	15
Reconnaissance/BM/C3I		
E-8	18	12
EC-130	7	3
WC-130	3	0
Total	28	15
Special OPS forces		
MC-130	4	4
Tanker		
HC-130	9	7
KC-135	226	172
Total	235	179
Transport		
C-5	30	27
C-17	8	8
C-21	19	2
C-26	11	0
C-32	2	0
C-38	2	2
C-40	3	0
C-130	173	165
LC-130	10	10
Total	258	214
Total Air National Guard	1,289	1,036

Source: "2008 USAF Almanac," *Air Force* (May 2008), p. 60.
a. That is, those in the force structure of operational units.

TABLE A-6. Age of U.S. Air National Guard Fleet

(as of September 30, 2007)

Type	Age in years									Total	Average
	0–3	3–6	6–9	9–12	12–15	15–18	18–21	21–24	24+		
A-10									1	105	106	26.8
C-5										30	30	35.7
C-17		8									8	3.5
C-21								2	17		19	22.5
C-26					9	2					11	13.3
C-32		2									2	4.2
C-38				2							2	9.5
C-40		3									3	4.3
C-130	7	10	14	22	34	33	11	25	50	206	19.2
C-135									226	226	47.1
E-8	1	5	7	4		1				18	7.5
F-15A-D								7	138	145	27.9
F-16			3	25	68	289	110			495	19.2
H-60				7		11				18	16.8
Total	8	28	21	31	75	104	313	160	549	1,289	25.7
Percent	1	2	2	2	6	8	24	12	43		

Source: "2008 USAF Almanac," *Air Force* (May 2008), p. 62.

TABLE A-7. ICBMs and Spacecraft in Service

(as of September 30, 2007)

Type of system	FY01	FY02	FY03	FY04	FY05	FY06	FY07
Minuteman III ICBM	500	500	500	500	500	450	450
MX "Peacekeeper" ICBM	50	50	23	6	0	0	0
Total ICBMs	550	550	523	506	500	450	450
DMSP satellite	2	2	2	2	2	2	2
DSCS satellite	5	5	10	11	9	9	9
DSP satellite (data classified)	—	—	—	—	—	—	—
GPS satellite	27	28	28	30	29	30	30
Milstar satellite	3	4	5	5	5	5	5
Subtotal military satellites, not including classified systems	37	39	45	48	45	46	46

Source: "2008 USAF Almanac," *Air Force* (May 2008), p. 62.

Notes

Chapter One

1. Steven M. Kosiak, "Costs of the Wars in Iraq and Afghanistan, and Other Military Operations through 2008 and Beyond" (Washington: Center for Strategic and Budgetary Assessments, 2008) (www.csbaonline.org/4Publications/Pub Library/R.20081215.Cost_of_the_Wars_i/R.20081215.Cost_of_the_Wars_i.pdf [January 30, 2009]), pp. iii, 6. Actual appropriations totals were $687 billion and $184 billion, respectively, based on partial appropriations for 2009. The figure for Iraq includes $32 billion in State and aid activities as well as $3 billion for Veterans Affairs; the figure for Afghanistan includes $13 billion for State and aid activities.

2. Speech of Secretary of Defense Robert M. Gates at the U.S. Global Leadership Campaign, Washington, D.C., July 15, 2008 (www.defenselink.mil/speeches/speech.aspx?speechid=1262 [August 1, 2008]).

3. Speech of Secretary of Defense Robert M. Gates, "The American Way of War," at the National Defense University, Washington, D.C., September 29, 2008 (www.defenselink.mil/speeches/speech.aspx?speechid=1279 [September 29, 2008]).

4. See, for example, Fareed Zakaria, *The Post-American World* (New York: W. W. Norton, 2008), pp. 87–128.

5. Those interested in such issues might consult, for example, the Brookings Institution's Global Economy and Development page (www.brookings.edu); David Sandalow's *Freedom from Oil: How the Next President Can End the*

United States' Oil Addiction (New York: McGraw-Hill, 2007); Bruce Jones, Carlos Pascual, and Stephen John Stedman, *Power and Responsibility: Building International Order in an Era of Transnational Threats* (Brookings, 2009), pp. 75–106, 234–67.

6. Office of Management and Budget (OMB), *A New Era of Responsibility: Renewing America's Promise* (Government Printing Office, 2009), p. 114.

7. Gordon Adams, "Secretary Gates Outlines Changes to Major Defense Weapon Systems" (Washington: Henry L. Stimson Center, April 6, 2009) (www.stimson.org/budgeting [April 9, 2009]).

8. See OMB, *A New Era of Responsibility,* pp. 54, 117–34.

9. See, for example, Mackenzie Eaglen, "Balancing Strategy and Budgets," *Armed Forces Journal* (October 2008): 12–19.

10. Gates, "The American Way of War."

11. Joby Warrick, "Experts See Security Risks in Downturn," *Washington Post,* November 15, 2008, p. A1.

12. Richard N. Haass, "What the Recession Means for Foreign Policy," *Wall Street Journal,* November 8, 2008, p. 11.

13. Congressional Budget Office, "The Long-Term Implications of Current Defense Plans: Detailed Update for Fiscal Year 2008," briefing slides (March 2008), p. 2 (www.cbo.gov/ftpdocs/90xx/doc9043/03-28-CurrentDefensePlans.pdf [July 5, 2008]).

CHAPTER TWO

1. William W. Kaufmann, *Assessing the Base Force: How Much Is Too Much?* (Brookings, 1992), pp. 21–22.

2. Secretary of Defense William S. Cohen, *Report of the Quadrennial Defense Review* (Department of Defense, May 1997), pp. x-xi.

3. Secretary of Defense Donald H. Rumsfeld, *Quadrennial Defense Review Report* (Department of Defense, September 30, 2001), p. iv (www.defenselink.mil/pubs/pdfs/qdr2001.pdf [July 28, 2008]).

4. Secretary of Defense Donald H. Rumsfeld, *Quadrennial Defense Review Report* (Department of Defense, February 2006), p. 3 (www.defenselink.mil/pubs/pdfs/QDR20060203.pdf [July 28, 2008]).

5. See also Scott Bates and Zachary Warrender, *Agility across the Spectrum: A Future Forces Blueprint* (Washington: Center for National Policy, June 2008), p. ix.

6. Michael J. Mazarr, "The Folly of 'Asymmetric War,'" *Washington Quarterly* 31, no. 3 (Summer 2008): 33–53.

7. Office of Management and Budget (OMB), *Historical Tables: Budget of the United States Government, Fiscal Year 2009* (Government Printing Office, February 2008), p. 137.

8. OMB, *Budget of the United States Government, Fiscal Year 2008: Historical Tables* (GPO, 2007), pp. 133–36.

9. International Institute for Strategic Studies (IISS), *The Military Balance 2008* (Oxfordshire, England: Routledge, 2008), pp. 443–49.

10. OMB, *Budget of the U.S. Government, Fiscal Year 2008: Historical Tables,* pp. 61, 79, 134–35.

11. Amy Belasco, "The Cost of Iraq, Afghanistan, and Other Global War on Terror Operations since 9/11" (Washington: Congressional Research Service [CRS], October 15, 2008), p. 10 (assets.openers.com/rpts/RL34473_20081006.pdf [November 25, 2008]).

12. See Under Secretary of Defense (Comptroller), *National Defense Budget Estimates for FY 2009* (Department of Defense, March 2008), pp. 80, 102.

13. IISS, *The Military Balance 2007* (Oxfordshire, England: Routledge, 2007), pp. 406–11.

14. IISS, *The Military Balance 2007,* pp. 357, 406–11; Office of the Under Secretary of Defense (Comptroller), *National Defense Budget Estimates for FY 2008* (Department of Defense, March 2007), p. 134.

15. National Commission on Terrorist Attacks upon the United States, *9-11 Commission Report* (GPO, July 22, 2004); Kathleen Ridolfo, "Iraq: Smuggling, Mismanagement Plaguing Oil Industry," Radio Free Europe/Radio Liberty (Washington, November 13, 2007) (www.rferl.org/featuresarticle/2007/11/38c235c1-6f71-46ac-9463-4119f5cb6fea.html [March 2, 2008]).

16. IISS, *The Military Balance 2007,* pp. 406–11; Office of the Under Secretary of Defense (Comptroller), *National Defense Budget Estimates for FY 2008,* pp. 214–15.

17. IISS, *The Military Balance 2007,* pp. 340–41; IISS, *The Military Balance 2008,* p. 376; Keith Crane and others, *Modernizing China's Military: Opportunities and Constraints* (Santa Monica, Calif.: RAND, 2005), pp. 101–03.

18. Department of Defense (DoD), *Military Power of the People's Republic of China, 2007: Annual Report to Congress* (Washington, 2007), pp. 25–29 (www.defenselink.mil/pubs/pdfs/070523-China-Military-Power-final.pdf [June 10, 2007]).

19. DoD, *Military Power of the People's Republic of China, 2008: Annual Report to Congress* (Washington, 2008), p. 32 (www.defenselink.mil/pubs/pdfs/China_Military_Report_08.pdf [March 10, 2008]).

20. Bruce Jones, Carlos Pascual, and Stephen John Stedman, *Power and Responsibility: Building International Order in an Era of Transnational Threats* (Brookings, 2009).

21. Speech of Secretary of Defense Robert M. Gates, "The American Way of War," at the National Defense University, Washington, D.C., September 29, 2008.

22. Richard K. Betts, *Military Readiness: Concepts, Choices, Consequences* (Brookings, 1995), pp. 115–43.

23. Heidi Golding and Adebayo Adedeji, *Recruiting, Retention, and Future Levels of Military Personnel* (Washington: Congressional Budget Office, 2006), p. 6; John Allen Williams, "Anticipated and Unanticipated Consequences of the Creation of the All-Volunteer Forces," in *The U.S. Citizen-Soldier at War: A Retrospective Look and the Road Ahead,* McCormick Tribune Conference Series (Chicago: McCormick Tribune Foundation, 2008), pp. 37–38.

24. Anita Dancs, "Military Recruiting 2007: Army Misses Benchmarks by Greater Margin" (Northampton, Mass.: National Priorities Project, January 22, 2008) (www.nationalpriorities.org/militaryrecruiting2007 [April 2, 2008]).

25. Michèle A. Flournoy and Alice E. Hunt, "The State of the U.S. Ground Forces" (Washington: Center for a New American Security, August 2008), p. 1.

26. Christian Davenport, "Downturn Drives Military Rolls Up," *Washington Post,* November 29, 2008, p. B1.

27. Lt. Col. Bryan Hilferty, "Information Paper: West Point Graduate Retention after 5-Year Active Duty Service Obligation" (New York: West Point, December 5, 2007).

28. U.S. Army, "U.S. Army Officer Retention Fact Sheet as of May 25, 2007," (Washington, May 25, 2007) (www.armyg1.army.mil/docs/public%20affairs/ officer%20retention%20fact%20sheet%2025may07.pdf [March 25, 2008]).

29. Stephen J. Lofgren, "Retention during the Vietnam War and Today," U.S. Army Center of Military History Information Paper (Washington: U.S. Army, February 1, 2008).

30. Michèle A. Flournoy, "Strengthening the Readiness of the U.S. Military," testimony before the House Armed Services Committee, 110 Cong. 2 sess., February 14, 2008, p. 3.

31. U.S. Army, "U.S. Army Officer Retention Fact Sheet as of May 25, 2007."

32. Heidi Golding and Adebayo Adedeji, *The All-Volunteer Military: Issues and Performance* (Washington: CBO, July 2007), pp. 14–17.

33. Ann Scott Tyson, "Military Waivers for Ex-Convicts Increase," *Washington Post,* April 22, 2008, p. A1.

34. Leslie Kaufman, "After War, Love Can Be a Battlefield," *New York Times,* April 6, 2008, p. ST1; Pauline Jelinek, "Military Divorce Rate Holding Steady," wtop.com, March 1, 2008 (www.wtopnews.com [April 1, 2008]).

35. Ann Scott Tyson, "Military Investigates West Point Suicides," *Washington Post,* January 30, 2009, p. A2.

36. Pauline Jelinek, "Army Suicides Highest in 26 Years," *washingtonpost.com,* August 15, 2007 (www.washingtonpost.com/wp-dyn/content/article/2007/ 08/15/AR2007081502027_pf.htm [April 1, 2008]); "Suicide Statistics," suicide.org (www.suicide.org/suicide-statistics.htm/#death-rates [April 15, 2008]); Associated Press, "U.S. Army: Soldier Suicide Rate May Set Record Again in 2008," *Examiner,* September 5, 2008, p. 12.

37. Thom Shanker, "Army Is Worried by Rising Stress of Return Tours," *New York Times,* April 6, 2008, p. A1.

38. For myself, in terms of policy recommendations, the above leads to three judgments: we waited too long as a nation to increase the size of the Army and Marine Corps after 2003, and we should keep increasing the size of the standing, active ground forces today even if we are belated in doing so; we do not have the luxury of increasing overall deployed force levels abroad now, relative to where they are in mid-2009, and in fact we should be trying to downsize, though the situation does not require this immediately as a matter of extreme urgency; and we owe it to our men and women in uniform to further improve compensation and other help for them and their families, even if benefits are already relatively robust overall.

39. Frances M. Lussier, *Replacing and Repairing Equipment Used in Iraq and Afghanistan: The Army's Reset Program* (Washington: CBO, 2007), pp. 1–15.

40. Robert F. Hale, *Promoting Efficiency in the Department of Defense: Keep Trying, But Be Realistic* (Washington: Center for Strategic and Budgetary Assessments, 2002), pp. ii–iii.

CHAPTER THREE

1. The matter of helping other countries with their nuclear security efforts is also important and is a topic to which I return in a later chapter on foreign assistance and diplomacy. Another worthy idea, a fissile material cutoff treaty, is not discussed here because of its relatively modest budgetary significance for the United States combined with this book's focus on budgetary matters. But there is a strong case for such an accord. On that, see Bruce Jones, Carlos Pascual, and Stephen John Stedman, *Power and Responsibility: Building International Order in an Era of Transnational Threats* (Brookings, 2009), pp. 107–38.

2. On the idea of major White House involvement, see Stephen J. Blank, *Russia and Arms Control: Are There Opportunities for the Obama Administration?* (Carlisle Barracks, Pa.: U.S. Army War College, Strategic Studies Institute, 2009), p. 120.

3. Rebecca Grant, "The Cyber Menace," *Air Force Magazine* (March 2009): 27.

4. See Steven Pifer, "Reversing the Decline: An Agenda for U.S.-Russia Relations in 2009," Foreign Policy Paper Series 10 (Brookings, January 2009) (www.brookings.edu [February 10, 2009]).

5. Robert S. Norris and Hans M. Kristensen, "Nuclear Notebook: U.S. Nuclear Forces, 2007," *Bulletin of the Atomic Scientists* (January–February 2007): 79–82; Robert S. Norris and Hans M. Kristensen, "Russian Nuclear Forces, 2008," *Bulletin of the Atomic Scientists* (May–June 2008): 55.

6. Steve Andreasen, "With Nuclear Weapons, A Lot Can Go Wrong?" *Minneapolis Star Tribune,* June 26, 2008.

7. Alexei Arbatov and Rose Gottemoeller, "New Presidents, New Agreements? Advancing U.S.-Russian Strategic Arms Control," *Arms Control Today* 38, no. 6 (July–August 2008): 10.

8. International Institute for Strategic Studies, *The Military Balance 2008* (Oxfordshire, England: Routledge, 2008), p. 29; Secretary of Energy Samuel W. Bodman and Secretary of Defense Robert M. Gates, "National Security and Nuclear Weapons in the 21st Century" (Department of Energy and Department of Defense, September 2008), p. 16 (www.defenselink.mil/news/nuclear weaponspolicy.pdf [September 25, 2008]).

9. Arbatov and Gottemoeller, "New Presidents, New Agreements? Advancing U.S.-Russian Strategic Arms Control": 12–14.

10. Amy F. Woolf, "U.S. Strategic Nuclear Forces: Background, Developments, and Issues" (Washington: Congressional Research Service, August 5, 2008) (http://assets.opencrs.com/rpts/RL33640_20080805.pdf [September 5, 2008]); Michael E. O'Hanlon, *The Science of War* (Princeton University Press, 2009), chapter 1.

11. Gordon Adams, "Secretary Gates Outlines Changes to Major Defense Weapon Systems" (Washington: Henry L. Stimson Center, April 6, 2009) (www.stimson.org/budgeting [April 9, 2009]).

12. Jayantha Dhanapala, "Rebuilding an Unraveled Consensus for Sustainable Nonproliferation," in *Breaking the Nuclear Impasse,* edited by Jeffrey Laurenti and Carl Robichaud (New York: Century Foundation, 2007), pp. 24–25.

13. See George P. Schultz, William J. Perry, Henry A. Kissinger, and Sam Nunn, "A World Free of Nuclear Weapons," *Wall Street Journal,* January 4, 2007, p. A15.

14. Anne-Marie Slaughter and others, *Strategic Leadership: Framework for a 21st Century National Security Strategy* (Washington: Center for a New American Security, July 2008), pp. 23–25 (www.cnas.org [July 25, 2008]).

15. For a good discussion along these lines, see George Perkovich and James M. Acton, *Abolishing Nuclear Weapons,* Adelphi Paper 396 (London: International Institute for Strategic Studies, 2008).

16. Thom Shanker, "Gates Gives Rationale for Expanded Deterrence," *New York Times,* October 29, 2008, p. A12.

17. Zhang Hui, "Revisiting North Korea's Nuclear Test," *China Security* 3, no. 3 (Summer 2007): 119–30.

18. Trevor Findlay and Andreas Persbo, "Watching the World," *Bulletin of the Atomic Scientists* (March–April 2005): 58–63.

19. David Hafemeister, "The Comprehensive Test Ban Treaty: Effectively Verifiable," *Arms Control Today* 38, no. 8 (October 2008): 8.

20. Steve Fetter, *Toward a Comprehensive Test Ban* (Cambridge, Mass.: Ballinger, 1988), pp. 107–58.

21. See Kurt M. Campbell, Robert J. Einhorn, and Mitchell B. Reiss, eds., *The Nuclear Tipping Point* (Brookings, 2004).

22. James Cotton, "North Korea and the Six-Party Process: Is a Multilateral Resolution of the Nuclear Issue Still Possible?" *Asian Security* 3, no. 1 (2007): 36–37.

23. "At the Workbench: Interview with Bruce Goodwin of Lawrence Livermore Laboratories," *Bulletin of the Atomic Scientists* (July–August 2007): 46–47.

24. National Nuclear Security Administration, "Reliable Replacement Warhead Program" (Washington, March 2007) (www.nnsa.doe.gov/docs/factsheets/2007/NA-07-FS-02.pdf).

25. Walter Pincus, "Gates Suggests New Arms Deal with Russia," *Washington Post,* October 29, 2008, p. A8.

26. Walter Pincus, "New Nuclear Warhead's Funding Eliminated," *Washington Post,* May 24, 2007, p. A6.

27. Michael A. Levi, "Dreaming of Clean Nukes," *Nature* 428 (April 29, 2004): 892.

28. National Nuclear Security Administration, "NNSA Budget, FY 2009" (Washington, 2008) (http://nnsa.energy.gov/management/nnsa_budget.htm [February 10, 2009]).

29. See Steve Fetter and Frank von Hippel, "Does the United States Need a New Plutonium-Pit Facility?" *Arms Control Today* (May 2004) (www.armscontrol.org/act/2004_05/fettervonHippel [September 22, 2008]).

30. Philip E. Coyle, "Oversight of Ballistic Missile Defense (Part 3): Questions for the Missile Defense Agency," testimony before the House Committee on Oversight and Government Reform, Subcommittee on National Security and Foreign Affairs, 110 Cong. 2 sess., April 30, 2008, p. 12 (www.cdi.org/pdfs/CoyleTestimonyApr08.pdf [July 29, 2008]).

31. "DoD News Briefing with Lt. Gen. Trey Obering," July 15, 2008, pp. 2–3 (www.defenselink.mil/transcripts/transcript.aspx?transcriptid=4263 [August 1, 2008]); Ronald O'Rourke, "Sea-Based Ballistic Missile Defense—Background and Issues for Congress" (Washington: Congressional Research Service, May 23, 2008), pp. 13, 40 (www.fas.org/sgp/crs/weapons/RL33745.pdf [August 1, 2008]).

32. Philip E. Coyle, "What Are the Prospects, What Are the Costs? Oversight of Ballistic Missile Defense (Part 2)," testimony before the House Committee on Oversight and Government Reform, Subcommittee on National Security and Foreign Affairs, 110 Cong. 2 sess., April 16, 2008, p. 21 (www.cdi.org/pdfs/CoyleHouseOversightGovtReform4_16_08.pdf [July 29, 2008]); Turner Brinton, "MDA to Order 19 More U.S. Ground-Based Interceptors in 2009," *Space News,* November 24, 2008, p. 12.

33. Missile Defense Agency, *Missile Defense Agency Fiscal Year 2009 Budget Estimates: Overview* (Department of Defense, January 2008), pp. 6–21 (www.mda.mil/mdalink/pdf/budgetfy09.pdf [July 29, 2008]).

34. Rear Admiral Alan B. Hicks, "Seabased Ballistic Missile Defense," *Joint Forces Quarterly* 50 (2008): 43–45.

35. Ann Scott Tyson, "U.S. Shoots Down Missile in Simulation of Long-Range Attack," *Washington Post,* December 6, 2008, p. A2.

36. Coyle, "What Are the Prospects, What Are the Costs?" pp. 17–18.

37. Warren Ferster, "Airborne Laser Conducts 1st Integrated Test Firing," *Space News*, September 15, 2008, p. 8.

38. Col. Robert McMurry and Lt. Gen. Michael Dunn, "Airborne Laser: Assessing Recent Developments and Plans for the Future" (Washington: George C. Marshall Institute, June 27, 2008) (www.marshall.org/pdf/materials/593.pdf [August 2, 2008]), pp. 1–9.

39. Walter Slocombe, undersecretary of defense for policy, "U.S. Limited National Missile Defense Program," presentation at Harvard-CSIS Ballistic Missile Defense Conference, Cambridge, Massachusetts, May 2000, p. 27; reprinted in *Defending America: The Case for Limited National Missile Defense,* James M. Lindsay and Michael E. O'Hanlon (Brookings, 2001), p. 6.

40. For a similar view, see Rep. Ellen Tauscher, "European Missile Defense: A Congressional Perspective," *Arms Control Today* 37, no. 8 (October 2007): 12.

41. George N. Lewis and Theodore A. Postol, "The Technological Basis of Russian Concerns," *Arms Control Today* 37, no. 8 (October 2007): 17–18.

Chapter Four

1. Edmund Cairns, *For a Safer Tomorrow: Protecting Civilians in a Multipolar World* (Oxford, England: Oxfam Publishing, 2008), p. 3.

2. See Gareth Evans, *The Responsibility to Protect: Ending Mass Atrocity Crimes Once and For All* (Brookings, 2008), pp. 31–50.

3. Anthony W. Gambino, "Congo: Securing Peace, Sustaining Progress" (New York, Council on Foreign Relations, October 2008), pp. 1–20 (www.cfr.org/content/publications/attachments/Congo_CSR40.pdf [October 31, 2008]).

4. Alix J. Boucher and Victoria K. Holt, "U.S. Training, African Peacekeeping: The Global Peace Operations Initiative (GPOI)" (Washington: Henry L. Stimson Center, July 2007), p. 3, (www.stimson.org/fopo/pdf/Stimson_GPOI_Issue_Brief.pdf [November 7, 2008]).

5. Current top troop contributors to the U.N. missions include Pakistan, Bangladesh, and India (each deployed nearly 10,000 troops in 2007); Nepal, Ghana, Jordan, Uruguay, and Italy (each 2,000 to 3,000); and Nigeria, Ethiopia, France, China, Morocco, Senegal, Brazil, South Africa, Benin, Spain, Indonesia, and Sri Lanka (each roughly 1,000 to 2,000). The largest missions were in the Congo, Liberia, Lebanon, Sudan, Ivory Coast, Haiti, Kosovo, and Ethiopia and Eritrea. The U.N. costs of these missions exceeded $5 billion a year. African countries provided about 16,000 troops, but missions on African soil required about 50,000 troops in 2007. As for non-U.N. missions, excluding Iraq but counting Afghanistan, top troop contributors were the United States (almost 17,000), the United Kingdom, Germany, Italy, and France (each 5,000 to 7,000); Canada, Russia, Turkey, and Nigeria (2,000 to 3,000 each); Australia, Rwanda,

Spain, Uganda, Poland, the Netherlands, Sweden, Hungary, Austria, Greece, and Romania (each roughly 1,000 to 2,000). The largest missions not including Iraq were in Afghanistan, Sudan, and the Balkans. In Iraq, to take a snapshot from late summer 2008 as the so-called surge of U.S. forces ended, the total force commitments were roughly 140,000 troops by the United States and just under 10,000 by all other foreign countries combined (4,000 U.K. forces, 2,000 personnel from Georgia, almost 1,000 from Poland, about 600 each from South Korea and Poland).

See Center on International Cooperation (CIC), *Annual Review of Global Peace Operations, 2008* (Boulder, Colo.: Lynne Rienner, 2008), pp. 139, 147–48, 164, 170, 180–355; Jason Campbell and Michael O'Hanlon, "Iraq Index" (Brookings, July 17, 2008) (www.brookings.edu/iraqindex [July 17, 2008]).

6. CIC, *Annual Review of Global Peace Operations, 2008*, pp. 2–4, 137–193, 195–355.

7. Government Accountability Office (GAO), *United Nations Peacekeeping,* GAO-09-142 (December 2008), p. 4.

8. Frederick Kagan and Michael O'Hanlon, *Bridging the Foreign Policy Divide* (New York: Routledge, 2008), pp. 70–75.

9. Madeleine K. Albright, William S. Cohen, and the Genocide Prevention Task Force, *Preventing Genocide: A Blueprint for U.S. Policymakers* (Washington: United States Holocaust Memorial Museum, 2008), p. 114; Stuart E. Eizenstat, John Edward Porter, Jeremy M. Weinstein, and the Commission on Weak States and National Security, *On The Brink: Weak States and U.S. National Security* (Washington: Center for Global Development, 2004), p. 4; Michael E. O'Hanlon, *Expanding Global Military Capacity for Humanitarian Intervention* (Brookings, 2003), pp. 70–74, 98–105.

10. Amy Belasco, *The Cost of Iraq, Afghanistan, and Other Global War on Terror Operations Since 9/11* (Washington: Congressional Research Service [CRS], June 23, 2008), p. 44.

11. See Samuel R. Berger, Brent Scowcroft, William Nash, and an Independent Task Force, "In the Wake of War: Improving U.S. Post-Conflict Capabilities" (New York: Council on Foreign Relations, 2005), pp. 36–37 (www.cfr. org/publication/8438 [July 1, 2008]); GAO, *Peacekeeping: Thousands Trained but United States Is Unlikely to Complete All Activities by 2010 and Some Improvements Are Needed,* GAO-08-754 (June 2008), pp. 1–48 (www.gao. gov/new.items/d08754.pdf [November 4, 2008]); O'Hanlon, *Expanding Global Military Capacity for Humanitarian Intervention,* pp. 98–105.

12. Although it is not of direct bearing on U.S. national security budgets, Europe for its part should collectively be capable of deploying and sustaining up to 200,000 troops in the field at a time, globally. Its capabilities at present are roughly half of that, and its average deployment totals over the last half decade have ranged from 60,000 to 70,000 personnel abroad at a time. Its current official goals as declared in NATO's Comprehensive Political Guidance from the

2006 Riga summit are roughly 130,000 to 150,000 deployable troops. This is the right general direction but not enough. Ideally, European defense budgets should grow to fund a further expansion. But an even greater and endemic problem is misplaced defense spending priorities—with too many forces equipped with too many tanks and fighters and warships, and not enough transportation assets or deployable logistics capabilities. France's latest defense streamlining plan, by which 54,000 military and civilian jobs would be cut to increase resources for power projection and other key capabilities, is a good example of the kind of reform that is needed. A detailed cost study of how to modify budget priorities is beyond the scope of this study. But the right modification of $20 billion worth of annual European spending could suffice to achieve the goals outlined above. For example, buying twenty large transport ships at $300 million apiece and 100 large airlift aircraft at $200 million apiece requires an investment of about $26 billion that if spread over ten years would be eminently within reach. European countries already have plans to purchase large numbers of transport aircraft, but they need to follow through. See Julian Lindley-French and Franco Algieri, *A European Defence Strategy* (Guetersloh, Germany: Bertelsmann Foundation, May 2004), p. 10; Bastian Giegerich, *European Military Crisis Management: Connecting Ambition and Reality*, Adelphi Paper 397 (London: International Institute for Strategic Studies, 2008), p. 46; Richard L. Kugler and Hans Binnendijk, *Toward a New Transatlantic Compact* (Washington: Center for Technology and National Security Policy, August 2008), p. 31; Tom Kington, "Italy Plans 6.9% Defense Budget Cut," *Defense News*, October 13, 2008, p. 1; Andrew Chuter, "U.K. Shuffles MoD Leaders," *Defense News*, October 13, 2008, p. 4; Michael A. Taverna, "Hardball," *Aviation Week and Space Technology*, July 28, 2008, pp. 32–33; Daniel Keohane and Tomas Valasek, *Willing and Able? EU Defense in 2020* (London: Centre for European Reform, 2008), pp. 27–36, 41–51.

13. GAO, *Force Structure: The Army Needs a Results-Oriented Plan to Equip and Staff Modular Forces and a Thorough Assessment of Their Capabilities*, GAO-09-131 (November 2008), pp. 11–13 (www.gao.gov/new.items/d09131.pdf [November 25, 2008]).

14. See Jason Campbell and Michael O'Hanlon, "The Iraq Index" (Brookings, November 6, 2008), p. 30 (www.brookings.edu/saban/~/media/Files/Centers/Saban/Iraq%20Index/index.pdf [November 25, 2008]).

15. For a concurring view, see the speech of Secretary of Defense Robert M. Gates, "The American Way of War," at the National Defense University, Washington, D.C., September 29, 2008.

16. Headquarters, Department of the Army, *Field Manual 3-07: Stability Operations* (Department of Defense [DoD], October 2008), p. vi (www.fas.org/irp/doddir/army/fm3-07.pdf [October 6, 2008]).

17. National Intelligence Council, *Global Trends 2025: A Transformed World* (Washington, 2008), p. 71.

18. For a review of some of the debate, see T. X. Hammes, "The Art of Petraeus," *National Interest* 98 (November–December 2008): 53–59.

19. Gates, "The American Way of War."

20. John A. Nagl, "Institutionalizing Adaptation: It's Time for a Permanent Army Advisor Corps" (Washington: Center for a New American Security, June 2007), pp. 3–8 (www.cnas.org [November 4, 2008]). For a related view, see Andrew F. Krepinevich, *An Army at the Crossroads* (Washington: Center for Strategic and Budgetary Assessments, 2008), p. xiii.

21. See U.S. Army, "Stability Operations in an Era of Persistent Conflict" (Carlisle Barracks, Pa.: U.S. Army War College, June 2008), p. 24 (www.carlisle. army.mil/ietcop/documents/Stability%20Operations%20in%20an%20Era%20 of%20Persistent%20Conflict%20(1%20Jun%2008).pdf [January 28, 2009]).

22. One suggestion to increase civil affairs brigades and psychological operations groups by three would be of roughly this magnitude—perhaps 3,000 personnel. See Robert Martinage, *Special Operations Forces: Future Challenges and Opportunities* (Washington: Center for Strategic and Budgetary Assessments, 2008), p. xiv.

23. Martinage, *Special Operations Forces,* pp. 52–68.

24. For similar ideas, see Lynn E. Davis and others, *Army Forces for Homeland Security* (Santa Monica, Calif.: RAND, 2004).

25. Carla Tighe Murray, *Evaluating Military Compensation* (Washington: Congressional Budget Office [CBO], 2007), pp. 1–20.

26. Steven M. Kosiak, *Military Compensation: Requirements, Trends and Options* (Washington: Center for Strategic and Budgetary Assessments, 2005), pp. 20–21; Cindy Williams, "Introduction," in *Filling the Ranks: Transforming the U.S. Military Personnel System,* edited by Cindy Williams (MIT Press, 2004), pp. 16–20; Paul F. Hogan, "Overview of the Current Personnel and Compensation System," in *Filling the Ranks,* pp. 49–51.

27. Lizette Alvarez, "New Veterans Hit Hard By Economic Crisis," *New York Times,* November 18, 2008.

28. GAO, *Defense Acquisitions: Assessments of Selected Weapons Programs,* GAO-08-467SP (March 2008), pp. 4, 5, 7 (www.gao.gov/new.items/d08467sp. pdf [June 25, 2008]).

29. John T. Bennett, "Advisers: Overhaul DoD Arms Buying," *Defense News,* October 27, 2008, p. 1.

30. GAO, *Defense Acquisitions: Assessments of Selected Weapons Programs,* pp. 5, 16.

31. Charlie Savage, "Senator Warns of a 'Crisis' in Pentagon Cost Overruns," *New York Times,* June 4, 2008.

32. Dana Hedgpeth, "Contracting Boom Could Fizzle Out," *Washington Post,* April 7, 2009, p. A1.

33. Philip Taubman, "Top Engineers Shun Military; Concern Grows," *New York Times,* June 25, 2008, p. A1.

34. GAO, *Defense Acquisitions: Assessments of Selected Weapons Programs,* p. 5.

35. John D. Moteff, "The Department of Defense Science and Technology Program: An Analysis, FY1998-FY2007" (Washington: CRS, September 12, 2008), p. 2 (www.assets.opencrs.com/rpts/RL34666_20080912.pdf [September 26, 2008]).

36. Sean Maloney and Christopher Thomas, "Strengthening U.S. Information Technology: Keep America No. 1 on the Net," in *Opportunity 08: Independent Ideas for America's Next President,* 2nd ed., edited by Michael O'Hanlon (Brookings, 2008), pp. 381–82. Maloney and Thomas propose 50,000 scholarships funded at $15,000 a year, for a total cost of $750 million annually.

37. Briefing by Lt. Gen. Raymond Johns Jr., U.S. Air Force, Washington, D.C., February 2008.

38. GAO, *Joint Strike Fighter: Progress Made and Challenges Remain,* GAO-07-360 (March 2007), p. 8 (www.gao.gov/new.items/d07360.pdf [June 25, 2008]); U.S. Air Force, *Fact Sheet: F-22 Raptor* (Washington, April 2008) (www.af.mil/factsheets/factsheet.asp?fsID=199 [July 23, 2008]). Were more F-22 planes purchased, production costs for additional planes would be less—perhaps around $120 million, for example, according to recent estimates. See Staff Sgt. C. Todd Lopez, "F-22 Excels at Establishing Air Dominance," *Air Force Print News Today,* June 23, 2006 (www.af.mil/news/story.asp?id=123022371 [July 23, 2008]).

39. See, for example, Christopher Bolkcom, "Navy-Marine Corps Strike-Fighter Shortfall: Background and Options for Congress" (Washington: CRS, August 1, 2008) (http://assets.opencrs.com/rpts/RS22875_20080801.pdf [September 10, 2008]).

40. GAO, *Joint Strike Fighter,* p. 18, 20.

41. Robert Wall, "Lightning Rod: USAFE Sees Fighter Modernization as Key to Its Role among Allies," *Aviation Week and Space Technology,* September 8, 2008, p. 57.

42. See CBO, "Cancel the F-35 Joint Strike Fighter and Replace with F-16s and F/A-18s," in *Budget Options* (Washington, 2007), p. 35; Steven M. Kosiak, *U.S. Defense Budget: Options and Choices for the Long Haul* (Washington: Center for Strategic and Budgetary Assessments, 2008), p. 46.

43. Gareth Jennings, "USAF Moves Ahead with Plans to Re-Wing Thunderbolt IIs," *Jane's International Defence Review* (July 2008), p. 22.

44. Christopher Bolkcom and William Knight, "Air Force Air Refueling: The KC-X Aircraft Acquisition Program" (Washington: CRS, August 4, 2008), pp. 29–37 (http://assets.opencrs.com/rpts/RL34398_20080804.pdf [September 9, 2008]).

45. Dakota L. Wood, *The U.S. Marine Corps: Fleet Marine Forces for the 21st Century* (Washington: Center for Strategic and Budgetary Assessments, 2008), p. xv; Michael E. O'Hanlon, *Defense Strategy for the Post-Saddam Era* (Brookings, 2005), pp. 90–91.

46. GAO, *Defense Acquisitions: 2009 Is a Critical Juncture for the Army's Future Combat System,* GAO-08-408 (March 2008), pp. 11–22, 41 (www.gao.gov/newitems/d08408.pdf, [June 30, 2008]).

47. That experimentation and learning process is of course well under way. For example, based on problems with excessive weight and rollover tendencies in early versions of the MRAP, subsequent purchases may emphasize somewhat smaller vehicles. (MRAPs have included vehicles such as the RG 33, Cayman, RG 31, Cougar, Buffalo, and MaxxPro.) See Kris Osborn, "U.S. May Buy Shorter, Lighter MRAPs," *Defense News,* July 21, 2008, p. 1. See also Andrew Feickert, "Mine-Resistant, Ambush-Protected (MRAP) Vehicles: Background and Issues for Congress" (Washington: CRS, August 1, 2008) (http://assets.opencrs.com/rpts/RS22707_20080801.pdf [September 10, 2008]).

48. "Statement of J. Michael Gilmore, assistant director, Congressional Budget Office, before the Subcommittee on Tactical Air and Land Forces, Committee on Armed Services, House of Representatives" (Washington: CBO, April 4, 2006), p. 17.

49. Ronald O'Rourke, *Navy DDG-1000 and DDG-51 Destroyer Programs: Background, Oversight Issues, and Options for Congress* (Washington: CRS, August 8, 2008), pp. 1–13 (http://assets.openers.com/rpts/RL32109_20080808.pdf [September 10, 2008]).

50. Christopher P. Cavas, "Cost Growth Kills another USN LCS," *Defense News,* October 13, 2008, p. 12.

51. Ronald O'Rourke, *Navy Littoral Combat Ship (LCS) Program: Background, Oversight Issues, and Options for Congress* (Washington: CRS, May 23, 2008), pp. 14–18 (www.fas.org/sgp/crs/weapons/RL33741.pdf [July 24, 2008]).

52. Eric J. Labs and Raymond Hall, *Resource Implications of the Navy's Fiscal Year 2009 Shipbuilding Plan* (Washington: CBO, June 9, 2008), pp. 8–9 (www.cbo.gov [July 24, 2008]).

53. Ronald O'Rourke, *Navy Force Structure and Shipbuilding Plans: Background and Issues for Congress* (Washington: CRS, June 10, 2008), pp. 3, 26 (www.fas.org/sgp/crs/weaons/RL32665.pdf [July 24, 2008]).

54. Labs and Hall, *Resource Implications,* pp. 2–3.

55. Labs and Hall, *Resource Implications,* p. 19.

56. Daniel Coats, Charles Robb, Michael Makovsky, and an Independent Task Force, *Meeting the Challenge: U.S. Policy toward Iranian Nuclear Development* (Washington: Bipartisan Policy Center, 2008), pp. xi–xii.

57. Peter Fromuth, "Pirates, Again," *Washington Post,* December 4, 2008, p. A21.

58. Eric J. Labs, *Crew Rotation in the Navy: The Long-Term Effect on Forward Presence* (Washington: CBO, October 2007), p. 17.

59. Labs and Hall, *Resource Implications,* p. 2.

60. Captain Bruce Lindsey, U.S. Navy, "Recapitalizing Too Early," *Proceedings,* January 2009, pp. 32–37; Captain Bruce Lindsey, U.S. Navy, "Low Rider," *Time,* November 13, 2006.

61. Craig Hooper, "A Poster Child for Next-War-Itis," *Proceedings,* November 2008, pp. 22–26.

62. Some of the following is drawn from a study conducted for the Center for a New American Security, specifically, Michael O'Hanlon, *Unfinished Business: U.S. Overseas Military Presence in the 21st Century* (Washington: Center for a New American Security, 2008).

63. Kent E. Calder, *Embattled Garrisons: Comparative Base Politics and American Globalism* (Princeton University Press, 2007), p. 35.

64. Secretary of Defense Donald Rumsfeld, "Foreword," in *Quadrennial Defense Review Report* (DoD, September 30, 2001), pp. iii–iv.

65. Specifically, the 2002 National Security Strategy says that the United States will "champion aspirations for human dignity; strengthen alliances to defeat global terrorism and work to prevent attacks against us and our allies; work with others to defuse regional conflicts; prevent our enemies from threatening us, our allies, and our friends, with weapons of mass destruction; ignite a new era of global economic growth through free markets and free trade; expand the circle of development by opening societies and building the infrastructure of democracy; develop agendas for cooperative action with other main centers of global power; and transform America's national security institutions to meet the challenges and opportunities of the twenty-first century." See President George W. Bush, *The National Security Strategy of the United States of America* (White House, September 2002), pp. 1–2 (www.state.gov/documents/organization/15538.pdf [June 10, 2005]).

66. Douglas J. Feith, undersecretary of defense for policy, "Strengthening U.S. Global Defense Posture: Report to Congress" (DoD, September 2004), pp. 4, 6.

67. Secretary of Defense Donald H. Rumsfeld, *Quadrennial Defense Review Report* (DoD, February 2006), pp. 2–3.

68. Feith, "Strengthening U.S. Global Defense Posture," p. 13.

69. Frances Lussier, *Options for Changing the Army's Overseas Basing* (Washington: CBO, May 2004), pp. 52, 54; GAO, *DoD's Overseas Infrastructure Master Plans Continue to Evolve,* GAO-06-913R (August 22, 2006), p. 15.

70. See Secretary of Defense Donald H. Rumsfeld, "Global Posture Review of the United States Military Forces Stationed Overseas," testimony before the Senate Committee on Armed Services, 109 Cong. 2 sess., September 23, 2004, p. 7.

71. Leo Shane III, "Transformation: Stateside Bases Prepare for Influx," *Stars and Stripes,* June 20, 2007 (www.stripes.com/article.asp?section=104&article=54363&archive=true); Charlie Coon, "Craddock Concerned EUCOM Lacks Troops for Primary Missions," *Stars and Stripes,* March 21, 2007 (www.stripes.com/article.asp?section=104&article=43460&archive=true).

72. See, for example, Thomas P.M. Barnett, *The Pentagon's New Map: War and Peace in the Twenty-First Century* (New York: G. P. Putnam's Sons, 2004), pp. 224–31.

73. Guam hosts or will soon host several submarines, roughly four Global Hawk UAVs at a time, several F-22 fighters on rotation, and other assets. See David A. Fulghum, "America's Far, Far West," *Aviation Week and Space Technology,* July 28, 2008, pp. 65–67.

74. For a similar view, see Bob Killebrew, "The Left-Hand Side of the Spectrum: Ambassadors and Advisors in Future U.S. Strategy" (Washington: Center for a New American Security, June 2007).

75. For one good account of how training Iraqi forces requires a substantial amount of the time and attention of American forces in Iraq, see John A. Nagl, "We Can't Win These Wars on Our Own," *Washington Post,* March 9, 2008, p. B4.

76. GAO, *Defense Management: Comprehensive Strategy and Annual Reporting Are Needed to Measure Progress and Costs of DoD's Global Posture Restructuring,* GAO-06-852 (September 2006), p. 2.

77. Al Cornella and others, *Overseas Basing Commission* (Arlington, Va.: Commission on Review of Overseas Military Facility Structure of the United States, May 2005), p. v.

78. Lussier, *Options for Changing the Army's Overseas Basing,* p. xiv.

79. Michael O'Hanlon, "Restructuring U.S. Forces and Bases in Japan," in *Toward a True Alliance,* edited by Mike Mochizuki (Brookings, 1997), p. 161.

80. With the fleet response program, the Navy no longer insists on scrupulously maintaining an absolutely continuous presence in the Mediterranean, Persian Gulf, and Western Pacific regions. Now it is more inclined to make deployments unpredictable, sometimes using more and sometimes less assets than before.

81. Eric J. Labs, *Increasing the Mission Capability of the Attack Submarine Force* (Washington: CBO, 2002), pp. xvii, 11–13.

82. Cornella and others, *Overseas Basing Commission,* p. 28.

83. See, for example, Ronald O'Rourke, "Naval Forward Deployments and the Size of the Navy" (Washington: CRS, November 13, 1992), pp. 13–23; William F. Morgan, *Rotate Crews, Not Ships* (Alexandria, Va.: Center for Naval Analysis, June 1994), pp. 1–9.

84. O'Hanlon, "Restructuring U.S. Forces and Bases in Japan," pp. 171–72.

85. GAO, *Defense Infrastructure: Opportunity to Improve the Timeliness of Future Overseas Planning Reports and Factors Affecting the Master Planning Effort for the Military Buildup on Guam,* GAO-08-1005 (September 2008), p. 26 (www.gao.gov/new.items/d081005.pdf [September 12, 2008]).

86. Michael E. O'Hanlon, *The Science of War* (Princeton University Press, 2009), chapter one.

87. President Bush probably overstated the morale benefits in his August 2004 speech on the subject. See Mike Allen and Josh White, "President Outlines Overseas Troop Cut," *Washington Post,* August 17, 2004, p. 1.

88. Michael R. Gordon, "U.S. Weighs Cutback in Forces in Germany," *International Herald Tribune*, June 4, 2004, p. 1.

89. General David McKiernan, then commander U.S. Army Europe, reportedly agrees with the idea of keeping two heavy brigades and effectively retaining a future Army troop strength in Europe at roughly the 2007 level. Some have simply favored slowing the redeployment, but rethinking and increasing the planned steady-state level seems the more appropriate response. See Nancy Montgomery, "General Casey: Slowing Europe Transformation Would Be the Right Decision," *Stars and Stripes*, October 27, 2007 (www.stripes.com/article. asp?sesction=104&article=57330&archive=true [November 1, 2007]).

90. Thom Shanker, "President Approves Realignment of the Army," *New York Times*, December 20, 2007.

91. For a related argument, see Cornella and others, *Overseas Basing Commission*, p. vi.

92. O'Hanlon, *Expanding Global Military Capacity for Humanitarian Intervention*, pp. 26–49, 67–74, 98–105.

93. For example, in countries with strong anticolonial traditions, anti-Americanism may hurt any indigenous government that associates too closely with the United States. It could in some cases help inadvertently strengthen insurgencies or terrorist groups as a result. See Dan Byman, *Understanding Proto-Insurgencies*, RAND Counterinsurgency Study Paper 3 (Santa Monica, Calif.: RAND, 2007), p. 28.

94. William E. Ward and Thomas P. Galvin, "U.S. Africa Command and the Principle of Active Security," *Joint Forces Quarterly* 51 (4th quarter 2008): 61–66.

95. Robert B. Oakley and Michael Casey Jr., "The Country Team: Restructuring America's First Line of Engagement," *Strategic Forum* 227 (Washington: National Defense University, Institute for National Strategic Studies, September 2007).

CHAPTER FIVE

1. Secretary of Homeland Security Michael Chertoff, "The Future of Homeland Security," speech at the Brookings Institution, Washington, D.C., September 5, 2008, p. 42 (www.brookings.edu/events/2008/0902_chertoff.aspx [September 24, 2008]).

2. Office of Management and Budget (OMB), *A New Era of Responsibility: Renewing America's Promise* (Government Printing Office, 2009), p. 72.

3. OMB, *Historical Tables: Budget of the United States Government, Fiscal Year 2009* (GPO, February 2008), pp. 142–43.

4. Steven M. Kosiak, "Overview of the Administration's FY 2009 Request for Homeland Security" (Washington: Center for Strategic and Budgetary Assessments, March 27, 2008), pp. 1–6 (www.csbaonline.org/4Publications/PubLibrary/U.20080330.FY_09_HLS_Request [September 15, 2008]).

5. Jennifer E. Lake and Blas Nunez-Neto, "Homeland Security Department: FY 2009 Appropriations" (Washington: Congressional Budget Office [CBO], September 25, 2008), pp. 9–10 (http://assets.openers.com/rpts/RL34482_2008 0925.pdf [October 20, 2008]).

6. Office of the Coordinator for Counterterrorism, "National Counterterrorism Center: Annex of Statistical Information," in *Country Reports on Terrorism 2007* (Department of State, 2008), p. 3 (www.state.gov/s/ct/rls/crt/2007 [June 1, 2008]).

7. Secretary of Homeland Security Michael Chertoff, "Confronting the Threats to Our Homeland," speech at Yale University, New Haven, Connecticut, April 7, 2008 (www.dhs.gov/xnews/speeches/sp_1208280290851.shtm [September 24, 2008]).

8. See, for example, Frank Hoffman, "Al Qaeda's Demise? Or Evolution?" *Proceedings,* September 2008, p. 21.

9. Department of Homeland Security (DHS), "TSA to Assume Watch List Vetting with Secure Flight Program," press release (October 22, 2008) (www. dhs.gov [October 22, 2008]).

10. Office of the Director of National Intelligence, "United States Intelligence Community Information Sharing Strategy" (Washington, February 22, 2008), p. 9 (www.dni.gov/reports/IC_Information_Sharing_Strategy.pdf [October 20, 2008]).

11. Jeremy Shapiro, "International Cooperation on Homeland Security," in *Protecting the Homeland 2006/2007,* Michael d'Arcy, Michael O'Hanlon, Peter Orszag, Jeremy Shapiro, and James Steinberg (Brookings, 2006), pp. 61–62.

12. Blake Harris, "Chicago Fusion Center Gives Police New Criminal Investigation Tools," govtech.com, April 21, 2008 (www.govtech.com/dc/articles/ 261463 [October 28, 2008]).

13. In this regard, the Department of Homeland Security's decision to loosen restrictions on how grant monies can be used—allowing, for example, up to half of all grants to be used for recurring personnel costs—is wise, because personnel costs are among the largest and most important homeland security expenses for states and localities. See Spencer S. Hsu, "Security Grants to Have Fewer Requirements," *Washington Post,* November 6, 2008, p. A6.

14. Department of Justice (DOJ), "Fact Sheet: Justice Department Counterterrorism Efforts Since 9/11" (September 11, 2008) (www.usdoj.gov/opa/pr/ 2008/September/08-nsd-807.html [October 20, 2008]); Federal Bureau of Investigation, "Protecting America Against Terrorist Attack: A Closer Look at the FBI's Joint Terrorism Task Forces" (December 1, 2004) (www.fbi.gov/page2/dec04/ jttf120114.htm [October 20, 2008]); John Rollins, "Fusion Centers: Issues and Options for Congress" (Washington: Congressional Research Service, January 18, 2008), pp. 2, 26, 30 (www.fas.org/sgp/crs/intel/RL34070.pdf [October 20, 2008]).

15. DHS, *Performance Budget Overview, Appendix C: Programs by Strategic Plan Goals* (2008), p. C-31 (www.dhs.gov/xlibrary/assets/budget_pboappc_fy 2008.pdf [September 15, 2008]).

16. David Heyman and James Jay Carafano, "Homeland Security 3.0: Building a National Enterprise to Keep America Free, Safe, and Prosperous" (Washington: Heritage Foundation and Center for Strategic and International Studies, September 18, 2008), p. 7 (www.csis.org/media/csis/pubs080918_homeland_sec_3dot0.pdf [September 28, 2008]).

17. Department of State, "The Electronic Passport: Frequently Asked Questions" (2008) (http://travel.state.gov/passport/eppt/eppt_2788.html?css=print [September 15, 2008]); John Leyden, "EPassport Tests Put Biometrics through Their Paces," *Register,* September 19, 2008 (www.theregister.co.uk/2008/09/19/eu_epassport_tests [October 10, 2008]).

18. DHS, "Fact Sheet: Electronic System for Travel Authorization (ESTA)" (June 3, 2008) (www.dhs.gov/xnews/releases/pr_1212498415724.htm [October 10, 2008]).

19. DHS, *Performance Budget Overview, Appendix C: Programs by Strategic Plan Goals,* pp. C-16, C-17.

20. Gregory F. Treverton, *Reorganizing U.S. Domestic Intelligence: Assessing the Options* (Santa Monica, Calif.: RAND, 2008), p. 60.

21. DHS, *Performance Budget Overview, Appendix C: Programs by Strategic Plan Goals,* p. C-7.

22. Chertoff, "The Future of Homeland Security," pp. 10–12.

23. Thomas X. Hammes, James A. Schear, and John A. Cope, "Protecting the American Homeland," in *Strategic Challenges: America's Global Security Agenda,* edited by Stephen J. Flanagan and James A. Schear (Washington: National Defense University Press, 2008), p. 96.

24. Stephanie Simon, "Border-Fence Project Confronts Obstacles," *Wall Street Journal,* February 4, 2009, p. A3.

25. DHS, *Performance Budget Overview: Fiscal Year 2008 Congressional Budget Justification* (2007), pp. 1–50 (www.dhs.gov/xlibrary/assets/budget_pbo_fy2008.pdf [September 15, 2008]); DHS, *Annual Performance Report, Fiscal Years 2007–2009* (2008), pp. 1–80 (www.dhs.gov/xlibrary/assets/cfo_apr_fy2007.pdf [September 30, 2008]).

26. Craig Whitlock, "Terrorism Financing Blacklists at Risk," *Washington Post,* November 2, 2008, p. A1.

27. Speech of Secretary of Homeland Security Michael Chertoff, "Addressing 21st Century Threats," Rice University, June 5, 2008.

28. DHS, *Performance Budget Overview, Appendix C: Programs by Strategic Plan Goals,* p. C-24.

29. OMB, *Budget of the United States Government, Fiscal Year 2009* (Government Printing Office, February 2008), pp. 69–73.

30. Col. David H. Gurney and Dr. Jeffrey D. Smotherman, "An Interview with Victor E. Renuart, Jr.," *Joint Forces Quarterly* 48 (1st quarter, 2008): 41; Gregory A.S. Gecowets and Jefferson P. Marquis, "Applying Lessons of Hurricane Katrina," *Joint Forces Quarterly* 48 (1st quarter, 2008): 74.

31. James Steinberg, "Intelligence Reform," in *Protecting the Homeland 2006/2007*, pp. 25–30.

32. Jeremy Shapiro, "Managing Homeland Security: Developing a Threat-Based Strategy," in *Opportunity 08: Independent Ideas for America's Next President*, 2nd ed., edited by Michael E. O'Hanlon (Brookings, 2008), p. 185; see also Glenn L. Carle, "Overstating Our Fears," *Washington Post*, July 13, 2008, p. B7.

33. For a concurring view, see Christine E. Wormuth and Anne Witkowsky, *Managing the Next Domestic Catastrophe: Ready (or Not)?* (Washington: Center for Strategic and International Studies, June 2008), p. x.

34. Wormuth and Witkowsky, *Managing the Next Domestic Catastrophe*, pp. 46–58.

35. Stephen Flynn, *America the Vulnerable: How Our Government is Failing to Protect Us from Terrorism* (New York: HarperCollins, 2004); Clark Kent Ervin, *Open Target: Where America is Vulnerable to Attack* (New York: Palgrave Macmillan, 2006).

36. Ervin, *Open Target*, p. 212; Michael d'Arcy, "Technology Development and Transportation Security," in *Protecting the Homeland 2006/2007*, pp. 140–42.

37. James Ott, "What Price, Cargo," *Aviation Week and Space Technology*, September 8, 2008, pp. 52–55.

38. I scale here using current levels of funding.

39. Transportation Security Administration, "TSA Proposes Large Aircraft Security Program," press release (DHS, October 9, 2008) (www.dhs.gov [October 10, 2008]).

40. Drew Griffin, Kathleen Johnston, and Todd Schwarzschild, "Sources: Air Marshals Missing from Almost All Flights," cnn.com, March 25, 2008 (www.cnn.com/2008/TRAVEL/03/25/siu.air.marshals/index.html [September 30, 2008]); Transportation Security Administration, "Federal Air Marshal Shortage?" (DHS, 2008) (www.tsa.dhs.gov/approach/mythbusters/fams_shortage.shtm [September 30, 2008]).

41. Michael d'Arcy, "Countermeasures against Specific Weapons," in *Protecting the Homeland 2006/2007*, pp. 170–76.

42. Gurney and Smotherman, "An Interview with Victor E. Renuart, Jr.," p. 42.

43. Randal C. Archibold and Andrew Becker, "Border Agents, Lured by the Other Side," *New York Times*, May 27, 2008.

44. Government Accountability Office (GAO), *Secure Border Initiative: Observations on Deployment Challenges*, GAO-08-1141T (September 10, 2008), pp. 1–20 (www.gao.gov/new.items/d081141t.pdf [September 20, 2008]).

45. OMB, *A New Era of Responsibility: Renewing America's Promise* (GPO, 2009), p. 72.

46. See Dana Priest and Amy Goldstein, "System of Neglect," *Washington Post*, May 11, 2008, p. A1.

47. U.S. Coast Guard, *U.S. Coast Guard Posture Statement 2009* (DHS, February 2008), pp. 15, 22, 32, 62 (www.uscg.mil/comdt/DOCS/LOW.RES.CG%20FY09%20Posture%20Statement.FINAL.Jan29.pdf [September 25, 2008]).

48. Lake and Nunez-Neto, "Homeland Security Department: FY 2009 Appropriations," p. 50.

49. "Safe Harbours," *Jane's Homeland Security Review* (October 2008): 22–27.

50. U.S. Coast Guard, *U.S. Coast Guard Posture Statement 2009*, p. 15; U.S. Coast Guard, "Budget in Brief, 2003" (February 2002) (www.dot.gov/bib2003/uscg.html [October 28, 2008]).

51. DHS, *Performance Budget Overview, Appendix C: Programs by Strategic Plan Goals*, p. C-27.

52. GAO, *Coast Guard: Observations on the Fiscal Year 2009 Budget, Recent Performance, and Related Challenges*, GAO-08-494T (March 2008), pp. 10–11 (www.gao.gov/new.items/d08494t.pdf [October 27, 2008]).

53. Peter Orszag and Michael O'Hanlon, "Protecting Infrastructure and Providing Incentives for the Private Sector to Protect Itself," in *Protecting the Homeland 2006/2007*, p. 84.

54. Lena H. Sun, "Metro to Randomly Search Riders' Bags," *Washington Post*, October 28, 2008, p. A1.

55. Mimi Hall, "Amtrak Expands Security Sweeps," *USA Today*, July 11–13, 2008, p. A1.

56. William Neuman, "More Delays for Cameras in Subways," *New York Times*, June 26, 2008, p. B1.

57. Richard A. Clarke, *Your Government Failed You* (New York: Harper-Collins, 2008), p. 258.

58. Michael Pan and others, "Safety Second," *New York Times*, August 8, 2004, p. WK11; Michael O'Hanlon, "The Roles of DoD and First Responders," in *Protecting the Homeland 2006/2007*, pp. 120–23.

59. State of Illinois, "Statewide Deployable Vehicles" (www.ready.illinois/gov/ittf/publications/StatewideDeployableTeams.pdf [October 25, 2008]).

60. DOJ, "Findings and Recommendations of the Suspicious Activity Report (SAR) Support and Implementation Project" (June 2008), pp. 1–7 (http://iwitnessvideo.info/files/mccarecommendation-06132008.pdf [October 31, 2008]).

61. Judith Miller, "On the Front Line in the War on Terrorism," *City Journal* (Summer 2007) (www.city-journal.org/html/17_3_preventing_terrorism.html [October 29, 2008]).

62. OMB, *A New Era of Responsibility*, p. 72.

63. Peter Orszag and Michael O'Hanlon, "Protecting Infrastructure and Providing Incentives for the Private Sector to Protect Itself," in *Protecting the Homeland 2006/2007*, pp. 80–81.

64. GAO, *Terrorism Insurance: Status of Coverage Availability for Attacks Involving Nuclear, Biological, Chemical, or Radiological Weapons*, GAO-09-39 (December 2008), pp. 1–9.

65. Among other things, the National Guard probably still should have greater representation at the United States Northern Command, and a number of planning efforts and exercises with other domestic and foreign actors merit further development. See James M. Castle, deputy director of interagency coordination for North American Aerospace Defense Command and U.S. Northern Command, "Supporting Homeland Partners," *Joint Forces Quarterly* 48 (1st quarter 2008): 44–50.

66. See Bert B. Tussing, "New Requirements for a New Challenge: The Military's Role in Border Security," in *U.S. Army War College Guide to National Security Issues, Volume II: National Security Policy and Strategy,* edited by J. Boone Bartholomees Jr. (Carlisle Barracks, Pa.: U.S. Army War College, Strategic Studies Institute, 2008), pp. 253–70.

67. Lynn E. Davis, and others, *Hurricane Katrina: Lessons for Army Planning and Operations* (Santa Monica, Calif.: RAND, 2007), pp. 54–58.

68. John T. Bennett, "McHale Seeks Funding for Emergency Response Teams," *Defense News,* July 28, 2008, p. 14; Gurney and Smotherman, "An Interview with Victor E. Renuart, Jr.," pp. 41–42.

69. Commission on the National Guard and Reserves, *Final Report to Congress: Transforming the National Guard and Reserves into a 21st-Century Operational Force* (Arlington, Va., 2008), p. 15.

70. OMB, *Budget of the United States Government, Fiscal Year 2009,* pp. 69–73.

71. GAO, *Biosurveillance: Preliminary Observations on Department of Homeland Security's Biosurveillance Initiatives,* GAO-08-960T (July 16, 2008).

72. J. Michael Barrett and Daniel Goure, "Chemical and Biological Threats: Surveillance as the First Line of Defense" (Arlington, Va.: Lexington Institute, 2008), pp. 12–16.

73. Gardiner Harris, "More Money for Food Safety Is Sought," *New York Times,* June 10, 2008, p. A15.

74. Peter Orszag and Michael O'Hanlon, "Protecting Infrastructure and Providing Incentives for the Private Sector to Protect Itself," in *Protecting the Homeland 2006/2007,* pp. 86–88.

75. Spencer S. Hsu, "Modest Gains against Ever-Present Bioterrorism Threat," *Washington Post,* August 3, 2008, p. A10.

76. Richard Danzig, *Preparing for Catastrophic Bioterrorism* (Washington: National Defense University, Center for Technology and National Security Policy, May 2008), pp. 22–45; on the broader importance of involving citizens in homeland security, see also Heyman and Carafano, "Homeland Security 3.0," p. 5; David Brown, "If Bioterrorists Strike, Letter Carriers Might Deliver Antibiotics," *Washington Post,* October 2, 2008, p. A2.

77. Hsu, "Modest Gains against Ever-Present Bioterrorism Threat," p. A10.

78. Joby Warrick, "Report Sounds Alarm Over Bioterror," *Washington Post,* November 30, 2008, p. A3.

79. See Brian D. Finlay, "Are We Safer?" *Baltimore Sun,* August 18, 2008.

80. Rita Grossman-Vermaas, Brian Finlay, and Elizabeth Turpen, *Old Plagues, New Threats: The Biotech Revolution and Its Impact on U.S. National Security* (Washington: Henry L. Stimson Center, 2008), pp. 44–47.

81. Flynn, *America the Vulnerable,* pp. 104–10.

82. Thomas B. Cochran and Matthew G. McKinzie, "Detecting Nuclear Smuggling," *Scientific American,* April 2008, pp. 98–104.

83. Josh Kussman and Brian C. Goebel, "Taking the Fight to the Cartels," *Washington Post,* April 4, 2009, p. A15.

84. See, for example, Stephen E. Flynn, "America the Resilient: Defying Terrorism and Mitigating Natural Disasters," *Foreign Affairs* 87, no. 2 (March–April 2008): 2–8.

85. Michael Chertoff, "Incomplete Security," *Armed Forces Journal* (October 2008), p. 44.

86. Spencer S. Hsu, "Plan to Fingerprint Foreigners Exiting U.S. Is Opposed," *Washington Post,* June 22, 2008, p. A8.

87. Lake and Nunez-Neto, "Homeland Security Department: FY 2009 Appropriations," pp. 74–77.

88. OMB, *A New Era of Responsibility,* p. 72.

89. DHS, *Performance Budget Overview, Appendix C: Programs by Strategic Plan Goals,* p. C-7.

90. Lake and Nunez-Neto, "Homeland Security Department: FY 2009 Appropriations," pp. 83–88.

91. Hammes, Schear, and Cope, "Protecting the American Homeland," p. 98.

Chapter Six

1. Lt. Gen. William B. Caldwell IV, commander, U.S. Army Combined Arms Center, "Foreword," in *Field Manual 3-07: Stability Operations* (Washington: Headquarters, Department of the Army, October 2008) (www.fas.org/irp/dod dir/army/fm3-07.pdf [October 6, 2008]).

2. Alternatively, or additionally, an interagency quadrennial national security review might be carried out—though it is likely already too late for that in the Obama administration. See Clark A. Murdock and Michèle A. Flournoy, lead investigators, *Beyond Goldwater-Nichols: U.S. Government and Defense Reform for a New Strategic Era, Phase 2 Report* (Washington: Center for Strategic and International Studies, July 2005), p. 28.

3. Nina M. Serafino, "Department of Defense 'Section 1207' Security and Stabilization Assistance: A Fact Sheet" (Washington: Congressional Research Service [CRS], May 7, 2008), p. 1.

4. Mark S. Martins, "The Commander's Emergency Response Program," *Joint Forces Quarterly* 37 (2005): 46–52.

5. Congressional Budget Office (CBO), "Analysis of the Growth in Funding for Operations in Iraq, Afghanistan, and Elsewhere in the War on Terrorism" (Washington, February 11, 2008), p. 6.

6. Cindy Williams and Gordon Adams, "Strengthening Statecraft and Security," Occasional Paper (Cambridge, Mass.: MIT, Security Studies Program, June 2008), p. 12; Sami Said and Cameron G. Holt, "A Time for Action: The Case for Interagency Deliberate Planning," *Strategic Studies Quarterly* 2, no. 3 (Fall 2008): 67.

7. Susan E. Rice, Corinne Graff, and Janet Lewis, "Poverty and Civil War: What Policymakers Need to Know," Global Economy and Development Working Paper (Brookings, December 2006).

8. Andrew Martin and Elisabeth Rosenthal, "U.N. Says Food Plan Could Cost $30 Billion a Year," *New York Times,* June 4, 2008 (www.nytimes.com [June 10, 2008]).

9. George E. Pataki, Thomas J. Vilsack, Michael A. Levi, David G. Victor, and an Independent Task Force, *Confronting Climate Change: A Strategy for U.S. Foreign Policy* (New York: Council on Foreign Relations, 2008), p. 8.

10. Susan B. Epstein and Kennon H. Nakamura, "State, Foreign Operations, and Related Programs: FY2009 Appropriations" (Washington: CRS, August 21, 2008), pp. 5, 30–35 (www.fas.org/sgp/crs/row/RL34552.pdf [October 24, 2008]).

11. Epstein and Nakamura, "State, Foreign Operations, and Related Programs," p. 20.

12. Office of Management and Budget (OMB), *A New Era of Responsibility: Renewing America's Promise* (Government Printing Office, 2009), p. 88.

13. Ibid., pp. 88–89.

14. Graham Allison, *Nuclear Terrorism: The Ultimate Preventable Catastrophe* (New York: Henry Holt, 2004).

15. Matthew Bunn, *Securing the Bomb 2007* (Cambridge, Mass.: Harvard University, Belfer Center for Science and International Affairs, September 2007), pp. 138–39 (www.nti.org/securingthebomb [June 15, 2008]).

16. Matthew Bunn, *Securing the Bomb 2008* (Cambridge, Mass.: Harvard University, Belfer Center for Science and International Affairs, 2008), p. xvii; Bunn, *Securing the Bomb 2007,* pp. 151–66. Of the 2006 nuclear-related funding of $1.1 billion, for example, about half was devoted to "Securing Nuclear Warheads and Materials," including the modified reactor fuel initiative and transportation security for nuclear materials and weapons transport in Russia; just over $200 million was for interdicting nuclear smuggling (largely through the Energy Department, also the top U.S. agency for relevant funding for the Securing Nuclear Warheads and Materials category); $100 million largely through State was for stabilizing employment for nuclear personnel overseas; and most of the rest, or nearly $200 million, was for ending further production of weapons-grade plutonium in Russia.

17. Bunn, *Securing the Bomb 2007,* p. 112.

18. Newt Gingrich, George Mitchell, and the Task Force on the United Nations, *American Interests and U.N. Reform* (Washington: U.S. Institute of Peace, 2005), pp. 77–84.

19. Gingrich, Mitchell, and the Task Force on the United Nations, *American Interests and U.N. Reform*, pp. 77–85.

20. American Academy of Diplomacy and Stimson Center Task Force on Resources for U.S. Global Engagement, "A Foreign Affairs Budget for the Future: Fixing the Crisis in Diplomatic Readiness" (Washington, October 2008), pp. 6–20 (www.stimson.org/pub.cfm?id=686 [October 21, 2008]).

21. Bruce Jones, Carlos Pascual, and Stephen John Stedman, "A Plan for Action" (Brookings, Managing Global Insecurity Project, 2008), p. 19.

22. Jeffrey D. McCausland, *Developing Strategic Leaders for the 21st Century* (Carlisle Barracks, Pa.: U.S. Army War College, Strategic Studies Institute, 2008), pp. 44–45.

23. Michael J. McNerney, "Stabilization and Reconstruction in Afghanistan: Are PRTs a Model or a Muddle?" *Parameters* (Winter 2005–06): 45.

24. American Academy of Diplomacy and Stimson Center Task Force on Resources for U.S. Global Engagement, "A Foreign Affairs Budget for the Future," pp. iii, 22.

25. Carol Bellamy and Adam Weinberg, "Educational and Cultural Exchanges to Restore America's Image," *Washington Quarterly* 31, no. 3 (Summer 2008): 55–68.

26. Juan Cole, *Engaging the Muslim World* (New York: Palgrave Macmillan, 2009), pp. 241–42.

27. Kristin M. Lord, "Voices of America: U.S. Public Diplomacy for the 21st Century" (Brookings, November 2008), p. 32. Student visitors to the United States, on average, have more positive views of the United States than others do, by about 10 percentage points. See Subcommittee on International Organizations, Human Rights, and Oversight, House Committee on Foreign Affairs, *The Decline in America's Reputation: Why?* (Government Printing Office, June 2008), p. 10.

28. Tamara Cofman Wittes, *Freedom's Unsteady March: America's Role in Building Arab Democracy* (Brookings, 2008), p. 147; Kenneth M. Pollack, *A Path Out of the Desert* (New York: Random House, 2008), pp. 296–98.

29. James A. Schear, "Defusing Conflicts in Unstable Regions," in *Strategic Challenges: America's Global Security Agenda,* edited by Stephen J. Flanagan and James A. Schear (Washington: National Defense University Press, 2008), p. 143.

30. J. Brian Atwood, M. Peter McPherson, and Andrew Natsios, "Making Foreign Aid a More Effective Tool," *Foreign Affairs* 87, no. 6 (November–December 2008): 123–32.

31. Paul Burton, "Developing Disorder: Divergent PRT Models in Afghanistan," *Jane's Intelligence Review* 20, no. 10 (October 2008): 30–33.

32. Seth G. Jones, *Counterinsurgency in Afghanistan* (Santa Monica, Calif.: RAND, 2008), pp. 130–33.

33. George S. Dunlop, "Economic Empowerment Tasks for Stability Operations," in *Stability Operations and State-Building: Continuities and Contingencies,* edited by Greg Kaufmann (Carlisle Barracks, Pa.: U.S. Army War College, Strategic Studies Institute, October 2008), pp. 180–213; Keith W. Mines, "The Economic Tool in Counterinsurgency and Post-Conflict Stabilization: Lessons Learned (and Relearned) in Al Anbar, Iraq, 2003–2004," in *Countering Insurgency and Promoting Democracy,* edited by Manolis Priniotakis (New York: Center for Emerging National Security Affairs, 2007), pp. 174–89.

34. Dennis R.J. Penn, "US Africom: The Militarization of U.S. Foreign Policy?" *Joint Forces Quarterly* 51 (4th quarter 2008): 75–76.

35. Terrence K. Kelly, Ellen E. Tunstall, Thomas S. Szayna, and Deanna Weber Prine, *Stabilization and Reconstruction Staffing: Developing U.S. Civilian Personnel Capabilities* (Santa Monica, Calif.: RAND, 2008), pp. 19–24.

36. Samuel R. Berger, Brent Scowcroft, William Nash, and an Independent Task Force, "In the Wake of War: Improving U.S. Post-Conflict Capabilities" (New York: Council on Foreign Relations, 2005), pp. 19–23; Seth G. Jones, Jeremy M. Wilson, Andrew Rathmell, and K. Jack Riley, *Establishing Law and Order After Conflict* (Santa Monica, Calif.: RAND, 2005), p. 132; Kurt M. Campbell and Michael E. O'Hanlon, *Hard Power: The New Politics of National Security* (New York: Perseus, 2006), pp. 113–18.

37. These are also the priorities cited by PRT team members. See U.S. House of Representatives Committee on Armed Services, Subcommittee on Oversight and Investigations, "Agency Stovepipes vs. Strategic Agility: Lessons We Need to Learn from Provincial Reconstruction Teams in Iraq and Afghanistan" (GPO, April 2008), p. 69 (www.armedservices.house.gov/pdfs/Reports/PRT_Report.pdf [November 1, 2008]).

38. American Academy of Diplomacy and Stimson Center Task Force on Resources for U.S. Global Engagement, "A Foreign Affairs Budget for the Future," pp. iii–iv.

39. Carlos Pascual, "Building Capacity for Stabilization and Reconstruction," testimony before the U.S. House of Representatives Committee on Armed Services, Subcommittee on Oversight and Investigations, 110 Cong. 2 sess., January 29, 2008 (www.brookings.edu [September 1, 2008]).

40. See Office of the Coordinator for Reconstruction and Stabilization, "Reference Guide to the President's FY 2009 Budget Request for the Civilian Stabilization Initiative" (Washington, 2008) (www.crs.state.gov/index.cfm?fuseaction=public.display&shortcut=4QJW [September 10, 2008]).

41. David C. Gompert and John Gordon IV, *War By Other Means: Building Complete and Balanced Capabilities for Counterinsurgency* (Santa Monica, Calif.: RAND, 2008), pp. 105–22.

42. Brookings Institution, "Compact between Scholars from the United States and the Muslim World," December 12, 2008 (www.brookings.edu).

43. Bruce Riedel, *The Search for Al Qaeda: Its Leadership, Ideology, and Future* (Brookings, 2008), p. 139.

44. OMB, "International Affairs Function 150 Summary and Highlights: Fiscal Year 2009 Budget Request" (Washington, February 2008), pp. 72–73 (www.state.gov/documents/organization/100014.pdf [October 25, 2008]).

45. Michael O'Hanlon and Mike Mochizuki, *Crisis on the Korean Peninsula* (New York: McGraw-Hill, 2003).

46. Carlos Elizondo and Ana Laura Magaloni, "The Rule of Law in Mexico: Challenges for the Obama Administration," in *The Obama Administration and the Americas: Agenda for Change,* edited by Abraham F. Lowenthal, Theodore J. Piccone, and Laurence Whitehead (Brookings, 2009), pp. 194–99.

47. William Booth and Steve Fainaru, "U.S. Aid Delays in Durg War Criticized," *Washington Post,* April 5, 2009, p. A1.

48. OMB, "International Affairs Function 150 Summary and Highlights," p. 74.

49. Barnett R. Rubin and Ahmed Rashid, "From Great Game to Grand Bargain," *Foreign Affairs* 87, no. 6 (November–December 2008): 30–44.

50. Jason Campbell, "PRT Situation in Afghanistan's Regional Command East," unpublished trip report (Brookings, April 2008).

51. Oxfam, "Afghanistan: Development and Humanitarian Priorities" (Washington, January 2008) (www.oxfam.org/uk/resources/policy/conflict_disasters/downloads/afghanistan_priorities.pdf [November 1, 2008]); Riedel, *The Search for Al Qaeda,* pp. 148–51.

52. Ashraf Ghani and Clare Lockhart, *Fixing Failed States: A Framework for Rebuilding a Fractured World* (Oxford University Press, 2008), pp. 217–18.

53. Government Accountability Office, *Combating Terrorism,* GAO-08-622 (April 2008), p. 11 (www.hcfa.house.gov/110/GAO041708.pdf [November 1, 2008]).

54. Caitlin Harrington, "US Plans to Upgrade Pakistan's Cobra Helos," *Jane's International Defence Review* 41 (November 2008): 24.

55. For a very good report along these lines, see Daniel Markey, *Securing Pakistan's Tribal Belt* (New York, Council on Foreign Relations, 2008), pp. 31–50.

56. Richard Armitage, Lee Hamilton, and the Pakistan Policy Working Group, "The Next Chapter: The United States and Pakistan" (Washington: U.S. Institute of Peace, September 2008), pp. 1-6 (www.usip.org [October 20, 2008]); Ashley J. Tellis, "Engaging Pakistan—Getting the Balance Right" (Washington: Carnegie Endowment, September 2008), pp. 5–6 (www.carnegieendowment.org [October 24, 2008]).

57. Karen DeYoung, "Pakistan Will Give Arms to Tribal Militias," *Washington Post,* October 23, 2008, p. A1; International Crisis Group, "Reforming Pakistan's Police" (Washington, July 2008), pp. ii–iii.

INDEX

Gates, Robert: communications satellite program and, 44; CTBT and reliable replacement warhead concept, 52; current state of U.S. military and, 30; downsizing of U.S. military in Europe, 97; increase in ground troops and, 14, 67; nuclear deterrence doctrine, 47; personnel systems and, 72; plan to cut back weapons systems, 7; as secretary of defense, 1, 10; weapons acquisition outsourcing and, 80. *See also* Defense, Department of
Gaza Strip, 139, 140
General equivalency degree (GED), 31
Genocide Prevention Task Force, 67
Georgia (country), 6
Germany, 23, 94, 97–98, 99
Global Peace Operations Initiative, 67, 68t
Global Posture Review (GPR), 90–94. *See also* Military issues
Gompert, David, 61
Government Accountability Office (GAO), 75, 80, 81, 143
GPR. *See* Global Posture Review
Guam, 92, 93, 94, 95–97
Gulf War (First Gulf War or Iraq War I [*1991*]), 33

Haass, Richard, 10
Hamas, 139, 140
Hawaii, 96
Hazardous materials, 123–24
Health and Human Services, Department of (HHS), 103
Hiroshima bomb, 48, 53
Hoffman, Bruce, 105
Homeland defense and security: agencies and functions of, 103, 104; aircraft and, 105, 108, 109, 112–14; airports and, 113; border patrol and, 114–15; budgetary issues, 8t, 18, 102–03, 104, 105–06, 111–12, 112, 113–15, 116, 117, 118, 119, 120, 121, 122, 123–25; chemical and

biological attacks, sensors, and antidotes, 108, 120–22; Coast Guard and sea borders, 115–16; communications and, 106, 117, 135; definition of, 101–02; international partners of, 121, 124; mass transit, 116–17; military and National Guard capabilities, 16–17, 73–74, 109, 119–20; personal identification, 108, 123–24; planning scenarios and, 110; police resources, 117–18; present state of, 103, 105–12; public places, 109, 118–19; recommendations, 111, 112–25; response and evacuation plans, 124; screening of cargo, 107, 108, 112, 116, 122–24; terrorism insurance and, 118, 121; terror watch lists, 107, 112–13; transportation and, 108, 109, 123–24; U.S. financial assistance, 124
Homeland Security Council (HSC), 109
Homeland Security, Department of (DHS), 5, 6, 102–03, 107, 110–11
House of Representatives (U.S.), 7
HSC. *See* Homeland Security Council
Humanitarian interventions. *See* Peacekeeping and humanitarian interventions
Hutus (Congo, Rwanda), 61

IAEA. *See* International Atomic Energy Agency
IGPBS. *See* Integrated Global Presence and Basing Strategy
Illinois, 117. *See also* Chicago
Immigration and Customs Enforcement, 103
Incident Management Planning Team, 110
India: active duty military of, 27; military spending of, 23; nuclear program of, 46, 49, 50; Pakistan and, 6; terrorism in, 103–04, 109; views of the U.S., 49
Infrastructure protection, 107